No Grid Survival Projec

[14 in 1] 1000 Days of Tried & Tested Strategies and DIY Projects to Conquer Any Crisis or Recession! | The Complete Self-Reliance Package

Devan Miles

Contents

⭐ YOUR FREE GIFT ⭐

Welcome to the "No Grid Survival Projects Bible" – Your go-to resource for mastering the art of self-sufficiency!

Embark on a transformative journey with our groundbreaking book, meticulously crafted to empower you with essential skills for thriving off the grid. Within the pages of this comprehensive manual, you'll unlock a wealth of knowledge designed to revolutionize your approach to self-reliance.

But there's even more – we've surpassed expectations by offering an exclusive companion ebook: **"The Best Survival DIY Projects**." This digital treasure trove includes a compilation of our most ingenious and effective projects, carefully curated to elevate your self-sufficiency game. **As a bonus, discover additional insights through accompanying instructional videos.**

Ready to revolutionize your survival skills? **Simply scan the QR code below** and unlock the gateway to unparalleled self-sufficiency. "The Best Survival DIY Projects" awaits – your key to mastering the art of survival starts here.

SCAN THE QR CODE TO DOWNLOAD THE BEST SURVIVAL DIY
PROJECTS Ebook + VIDEOS

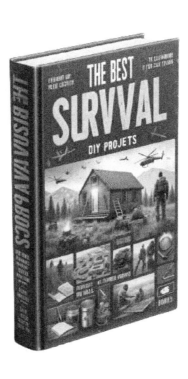

Introduction

Attempting to live independently from society's infrastructure may seem like a foreign and unneeded concept in today's interconnected world. However, it is impossible to overestimate the value of learning to thrive independently. The dangers in this interconnected web become more evident as our reliance on technology, infrastructure, and centralized services increases.

Being self-sufficient in the face of adversity or an emergency gives us a sense of invaluable strength and fortitude. The normal operation of our cities and towns can be disrupted by natural disasters, power outages, or even economic upheavals, leaving us vulnerable to the impacts of these events. Those who are prepared for such times with the knowledge and skills to survive off the grid will be in a better position than those who are not.

Adopting an off-grid lifestyle encourages a closer relationship with nature and the resources it provides. Learning how to exploit natural resources responsibly is crucial for lowering human environmental impact and fostering long-term viability. Insights like these inspire a concern for the planet's future and the protection of its natural resources.

In addition, self-sufficiency is frequently found in communities where people choose to live off the grid. People become less dependent on consumerism and commercial products when they acquire skills in farming, hunting, foraging, and do-it-yourself methods. Making a mental shift like this can help one become more financially secure, less wasteful, and more fulfilled.

The capacity to live independently of the grid also fosters a deeper sense of belonging and cooperation among its members. Together, people who pool their strengths and support one another create strong communities that can withstand adversity. This shared feature facilitates relationships characterized by trust and a sense of belonging, qualities that might be elusive in a modern, highly interdependent society.

Finally, learning to live alone offers a chance for introspection and a return to a more fundamental way of life. It's a great way for people to escape the hustle and bustle of everyday life, reconnect with nature, and go back to basics. This return to fundamentals has the potential to bring us great feelings of satisfaction, contentment, and fulfillment.

Living independently from the grid is crucial because it helps us maintain a sense of equilibrium. While modern life has many advantages, it also leaves us vulnerable in ways we can't always prevent. The experience of living off the grid provides us with the tools, knowledge, and perspective necessary to adopt a more independent, sustainable, and interconnected lifestyle. Aside from providing peace of mind in dangerous situations, this information can help us learn more about who we are and how we fit into the world.

The bedrock of off-the-grid sustainability is competence in the five pillars of survival: housing, water, food production, medicine, and hunting.

The need for shelter becomes critical in the most basic sense of the word. Forging shelter from natural materials or using eco-friendly construction allows individuals to create a weatherproof haven in tune with its natural surroundings, giving them a strong feeling of belonging.

The success of any off-grid endeavor depends on access to potable water. You can always access clean water by collecting rainwater, using springs, or using filtration. The search for water can be crucial to your survival, so it's important to know how to read the landscape and predict the weather to find the best water sources.

The ability to grow one's food symbolizes self-sufficiency, and food production is a dance with the rhythm of nature. Taking care of one's food supply by cultivating organic crops, pruning fruit trees, and tending to vegetable gardens is a satisfying experience. The delicate balance between humans and their environment is maintained by permaculture, in which crops and livestock mutually support one another.

Medicine, the protector of health, requires familiarity with herbal medicines and treatments. Without access to Western medicine, local herbs, and other alternative medicine have become increasingly important for curing illness and keeping people well. These all-natural cures testify to the inextricable link between people and their natural environment.

Hunting is an old survival dance that requires one to develop primal impulses and environmental consciousness. Traditional hunting methods passed down with utmost respect help maintain a healthy ecosystem by maintaining a balance in animal populations. Future generations can enjoy the rich tapestry of life by learning to hunt in a way that doesn't deplete natural resources.

A community can rely on and appreciate the natural world through a harmonious interplay of shelter, water supplies, food production, medicine, and hunting. An off-the-grid lifestyle is enriched by autonomy, sustainability, and a deep connection to the natural world when these core elements harmonize harmoniously. By embodying these ageless abilities, people can gracefully face life's obstacles, passing on the tradition of survival and harmony with the natural world to future generations.

If you want to learn everything you need to know to survive in an off-the-grid setting, this book is your best bet. It teaches readers to be self-sufficient and robust by covering shelter, water sources, food production, medicine, and hunting.

As a first step, the manual provides priceless advice on building a safe haven that is weatherproof and in harmony with its surroundings. Readers will better understand how to construct using sustainable methods and materials found in their immediate area.

Second, knowing where and how to get water becomes critical information for those living off the grid. This article examines several water collection, purification, and conservation methods to provide a steady and safe water supply, even without modern infrastructure.

Another pillar takes shape as the guide teaches its readers how to raise crops and animals without upsetting the delicate ecological balance. Readers will learn how to design food production systems based on permaculture principles that are self-sufficient and in tune with natural rhythms.

The guide also explores the field of medicine, revealing the efficacy of herbal cures and other alternative treatments. Individuals can care for their health without relying entirely on contemporary drugs if they learn about and engage with ancient healing traditions and understand indigenous plants' medicinal capabilities.

Finally, the guide provides insight into hunting, stressing the importance of balancing humane and ecological concerns. Readers will develop a profound understanding of the interdependence of all life forms and acquire the skills necessary to hunt in a way that protects wildlife populations and biodiversity.

The fundamental relationship between humans and nature is the central theme of this guide. Living in harmony with nature and appreciating the precarious equilibrium that allows life on Earth are emphasized. People can get closer to their environment and become more environmentally responsible if they adopt the ideas offered in this guide.

The information in the book helps readers see that they are not apart from nature but rather a vital cog in the vast, interconnected web of life. People's perspectives on the environment shift from exploiting it as a resource to treating it as a living, breathing organism worthy of care and respect due to this newfound humility and awe.

Readers will get a deeper understanding of the tremendous impact of their choices on the ecosystem as they delve into the complexities of shelter construction utilizing sustainable materials and eco-friendly procedures. Eventually, you understand that your every move affects the natural world and its precarious equilibrium. This realization motivates people to look for options that reduce environmental impact and safeguard the planet's natural beauty for future generations.

Similarly, as readers learn about different water collection, purification, and conservation techniques, they grasp this limited resource's vitality. The importance of water conservation and the need to protect water supplies from pollution and waste are stressed throughout the book. As a result of their newfound knowledge, people become responsible water stewards who value water for its vitality and work to protect it.

Exploring the world of food production allows readers to see the intimate relationship between the land and the food they eat. The environmental implications of modern agriculture, such as deforestation and chemical contamination, are highlighted throughout the book. With this information, farmers will be more likely to choose organic and sustainable methods, lessening their environmental impact and bolstering biodiversity.

The awareness of nature's healing potential is strengthened by the guide's examination of natural remedies and herbal knowledge for medicine. Understanding the interdependence of humans and the plant kingdom teaches readers how nature may treat illness and improve health. This knowledge instills a sense of duty to safeguard natural environments and preserve plant diversity for future generations' access to nature's healing bounty.

Last, the guide's suggestions for moral and environmentally sound hunting techniques provide new insight into our longstanding relationship with the natural world. Hunters teach their audience to respect the natural world and the cycle of life and death rather than seeing hunting as a sport or a means of conquest. This thinking fosters a deep appreciation for wildlife and the ecosystems they depend on, encouraging people to take action in defense of the natural world.

The fundamental message of the guide, however, goes much beyond ordinary survival methods, one of harmony with nature and environmental responsibility. It motivates a dramatic mental transformation, leading people to adopt a more aware, empathetic, and Earth-friendly way of living. Adopting the advice in this book would not only ensure one's independence from modern conveniences but will also make one a force for good in the world, helping to create an environment where people and wildlife can live in peace and harmony.

This book will give its readers the knowledge and skills they need to survive in harsh, off-the-grid conditions. Individuals can choose a way of life that promotes self-reliance, sustainability, and a profound respect for the complicated web of life by learning the essentials of shelter, water sources, food production, medicine, and hunting. By following the advice in this guide, readers can learn to live independently of the grid and help create a better, more peaceful world for themselves and future generations.

How To Can You Help This book?

Composing this book has proven to be quite a challenge in fact, debugging for hours feels easier than the process of writing. For the first time in my life, I've encountered writer's block. Understanding the topics is one thing, but attempting to articulate them in a logical, concise, cohesive, and well-organized manner is an entirely different task.

Furthermore, since I've chosen to steer clear of any publishing houses, I can proudly label myself as an "independent author." This is a personal decision that hasn't been without its difficulties, but my dedication to helping others has prevailed.

That's why I would be immensely grateful if you could provide feedback on Amazon. Your input would mean a great deal to me and would go a long way in sharing this material with others. I recommend the following:

1. **If you haven't already, scan the QR code** at the start of the book and download THE BEST SURVIVAL DIY PROJECTS eBook + VIDEOS.

2. **Scan the QR code below and quickly leave feedback on Amazon!**

SCAN ME

The optimal approach? Share a short video where you discuss your thoughts on the book! If that feels like too much, there's absolutely no pressure. Providing feedback along with a couple of photos of the book would still be greatly appreciated!

Note: There's no obligation whatsoever, but it would be immensely valued!

I'm thrilled to embark on this journey with you. Are you prepared to delve in?

Enjoy your reading!

Book 1:

Shelter and Accommodation

In the context of off-grid survival, shelter, and accommodation are fundamental to feeling safe and living in harmony with nature. More than just a roof over one's head, shelter is the skill of designing a space that allows one to feel at home with nature while protecting its residents from the elements.

The capacity to build a haven in the wilderness is a testament to people's resourcefulness and creativity in the face of nature's constant transformation. It demonstrates human ingenuity, originality, and appreciation for nature's bounty. When we set out to construct a home, we must discover the land's rhythms and contours, as well as the mutually beneficial interaction between architecture and its setting.

In contrast, accommodation refers to transforming a functional dwelling into a cozy abode that truly reflects its owners' personalities and objectives. It's a haven for the mind, body, and soul. Building an off-grid home from sustainable materials like wood, stone, or earth makes it feel like an organic part of the landscape. The distinction between the natural world and the comforts of home begins to blur as the shelter becomes one with the environment.

The conventional idea of lodging changes in this off-the-grid society. Houses are not built according to predetermined plans but take their cues from the landscape, shift with the seasons, and incorporate features from the surrounding environment. Rainwater is collected on the roof and replenishes supplies inside the house. The strategically placed windows let in natural sunlight, which warms the room. Eco-friendly insulation materials welcome the winter chill to keep you safe, while summer breezes are well appreciated.

More than just a roof over one's head, "shelter" encompasses much more here. Maintaining peace with one's natural environment is also a goal. People who live off the grid do so with a keen awareness of the ecosystem they occupy, knowing that their actions can significantly impact the ecosystem's delicate balance.

Living comfortably off the grid involves prioritizing simplicity and being in the present moment. It's a chance to disconnect from technology and reconnect with nature, the things that truly matter in life. Being at one with nature's cycles helps us appreciate the benefits of a minimalist lifestyle and rediscover the joy of having less stuff.

In conclusion, off-grid housing options capture the spirit of a life in harmony with the natural world. It's a form of creativity that considers long-term viability and ecological consciousness. By constructing a dwelling in harmony with its surroundings and making provisions that strengthen our bond with the earth, we generate a profound sense of belonging and learn that the wilderness can provide us with more than simply a place to sleep.

Building Temporary and Permanent Shelters

Constructing short-term and long-term shelters illustrates the inherent tension between flexibility and stability in off-the-grid living. Different kinds of homes are suited to various people and situations, and they all showcase the resourcefulness and creativity of their occupants.

In terms of flexibility and portability, temporary shelters are unparalleled. Shelters like this, made from lightweight, easily sourced materials, are designed to be quickly set up and taken down, making them perfect for transient or nomadic lives. The adaptability of temporary shelters is invaluable when unexpected weather or the need to relocate must be handled. The close connection between humans and their natural surroundings is reflected in the fact that these objects are often crafted ingeniously from natural resources like branches, leaves, and animal skins.

The skill of constructing makeshift homes resides in the rapidity with which one can assess the area and use its resources. To create yurts, teepees, or just plain lean-tos that blend in with their environment, nomadic people have developed these abilities for decades. These shelters offer instant cover from the elements during emergencies or exploratory expeditions without cutting off all contact with nature.

However, permanent shelters represent the permanence and steadiness that are aimed for in off-the-grid communities. These fortifications are built to last a long time and are made of durable materials like wood, stone, or dirt. Permanent housing requires more detailed design and planning, using up-to-date architectural knowledge and eco-friendly building practices.

Building a home that will endure a lifetime in the wild is a strong statement about one's dedication to eco-friendly living. Permanent residents deepen their ties to the land by designing structures that honor the spirit of the surrounding environment. To minimize their impact on the environment and highlight the elegance of organic architecture, these shelters frequently appear to be growing out of the ground.

Off-the-grinders looking for a more permanent solution may turn to earthbag building, straw bale walls, or passive solar architecture. They use local resources with an eye toward sustainability, understanding that a home's construction shouldn't negatively impact the ecosystem it's meant to coexist with.

The relationship between humans and their natural environments is crucial to off-grid survival, whether the goal is temporary or long-term housing. Both traditional wisdom influences these homes passed down through the ages and the understanding of indigenous tribes, as well as cutting-edge sustainable building practices. Both types of homes represent the bravery to go against the grain and chart a course that respects the planet's natural resources and promotes a more sustainable, communal way of living.

In conclusion, the skills required for off-grid survival, such as making temporary and permanent shelters, reflect the essence of flexibility and stability. It's proof that people can be strong and creative when they set out to live in peace and harmony with the natural world. These dwellings, whether made of lightweight materials for nomadic wanderings or planned with a vision of rooted stability, represent the timeless relationship between humans and their natural surroundings, where human creativity meets the ever-changing tapestry of nature.

Utilizing Natural and Recycled Materials

In the world of off-the-grid survival, using natural and recycled materials exemplifies the ethos of sustainable living and resourcefulness. This method exemplifies humanity's potential to live harmoniously with the natural world while reducing its ecological footprint.

By using natural resources, we are accepting the treasures our planet has to offer. Every material we use to construct our homes, from lumber and stone to clay and bamboo, has special properties. These materials not only help you feel more at one with nature, but they also help you blend in with the landscape.

Working in harmony with nature is the key to mastering the use of natural resources. We avoid depleting natural habitats and upsetting ecological equilibrium by carefully picking locally available, sustainable resources. Our decision to source resources close to home exemplifies the concepts of self-sufficiency and environmental stewardship.

Using natural and repurposed materials demonstrates our dedication to originality and mindfulness in daily life. We can reduce our environmental impact by giving previously useless things a new purpose or recycling building materials. As a result, the environmental toll of resource extraction and manufacturing is lessened, and landfills can hold less garbage.

Our off-grid homes are more interesting because of the recycled materials we've used to build them. Our buildings tell inspiring stories of sustainability and creativity by incorporating reclaimed materials such as wood, metal, and glass. We discover utility and beauty in these repurposed materials, building houses that are monuments to the efficacy of mindful existence.

Moreover, making something from scratch using only natural and recyclable resources encourages independence and innovation. It forces us to question the status quo and consider alternatives to factory-made goods. This method equips us with the skills of designers and artisans, allowing us to shape our homes while maintaining a close relationship with nature.

Using only renewable and recyclable materials in our off-grid home has given us a newfound respect for the natural world. We acknowledge that the natural world supplies many raw materials just waiting to be fashioned into the buildings that house our hopes and desires.

In conclusion, living off the grid using only natural and repurposed materials is a magnificent example of harmony between humans and the natural world. It proves we can live harmoniously with nature while appreciating its many gifts. By making this deliberate decision, we are demonstrating our dedication to sustainability, resourcefulness, and the art of crafting dwellings that provide us with safety and security and reflect the very essence of life itself.

1. **If you haven't already done so, scan the QR code at the beginning of the book** and download THE BEST SURVIVAL DIY PROJECTS eBook + VIDEOS.

2. **Scan the QR code below and leave quick feedback on Amazon!**

SCAN ME

Book 2:

Water Sourcing and Purification

Finding and purifying water is essential for off-grid survival, as it ensures a constant supply of drinkable water even while far from civilization. Understanding the complexities of water sourcing and purification becomes crucial in the quest for self-sufficiency, as water is essential to life and the bedrock of every thriving community.

Understanding the environment and its hydrological patterns is the first step in water sourcing. Those who live off the grid must closely monitor their surroundings to locate water sources like springs, streams, and underground aquifers. They learn to interpret natural markers, such as the proliferation of specific plant life or the shape of the terrain, as clues to the existence of water.

Many off-grid populations are turning to collecting rainwater as a reliable water supply. By collecting rainwater during wetter seasons, either from rooftops or catchment areas, people can store a significant amount of water used in the dry seasons. Taking advantage of nature's cycles this way is a model of efficiency and sustainability.

Nevertheless, obtaining water is only half the problem. Knowing how to purify water is essential for ensuring its viability for human consumption. People living off the grid are aware that if surface water is readily available, it may be contaminated with hazardous organisms. Therefore, cleansing acts as a preventative measure for physical and mental well-being.

Sedimentation and filtering via sand or gravel are two examples of natural purification processes used to eliminate bigger particles and other contaminants. The age-old practice of sterilizing water by boiling it over an open flame is an efficient way to remove harmful bacteria and other contaminants.

More advanced off-grid systems use water purifiers using activated carbon or ceramic filters to produce potable water. Together, these techniques represent the best of both traditional knowledge and cutting-edge research, giving people the confidence they need to face the problems of water purification head-on.

Water treatment goes beyond mere hygiene and into the realm of ecological responsibility. Because of their awareness of the importance of water to all living things, people who live off the grid take great care to protect these resources from pollution and contamination.

The necessity of water sources and purification for off-grid existence exemplifies the delicate tango between humans and the natural world. Clean water is always available because of the research and techniques pioneered in these fields, promoting ecological harmony. Off-grid communities guarantee their existence and celebrate the sanctity of water as a valuable life-giving resource by tuning into the cycles of the land, using the gifts of rain and the earth, and protecting water sources from harm.

Collecting Water from Natural Resources

An important part of learning how to survive off the grid is learning how to collect water from natural sources so that you may have a steady water supply without relying on municipal systems. Reading the land and its hydrological cycles to harness the abundance of water supplied by the natural world, this activity exemplifies the balance between humans and nature.

Rainwater harvesting is a common technique for acquiring water from the environment. Off-grid residents strategically place catchment systems, such as rooftops or specially constructed buildings, to collect rainfall during storms. Rainwater is channeled into reservoirs or storage tanks for later use. This method makes the most of what nature provides and decreases the demand for water from elsewhere.

Alternatively, gravity-fed systems can gather water in areas with readily available streams and rivers. To provide a constant water supply for daily needs, channels or pipelines are built to divert water from various sources to collection stations. Off-grid settlements make the most of these systems by conforming to the topography, reducing the need for energy-intensive pumps and other machinery.

Other useful natural resources for water gathering include wells and springs. Wells, either dug by hand or drilled, retrieve water from the earth as necessary. To maintain a steady supply of pure water, springs are carefully preserved and regulated at the point where water naturally emerges from the ground.

"Fog harvesting" techniques are used in areas with low natural water tables. Mesh nets or screens are used in these systems and are carefully positioned in regions prone to fog and mist. These nets allow fog to pass through, condensing the moisture into droplets that fall on the surface and eventually trickle down into containers below.

Getting water from natural sources is more than just taking what you need; it's also about stewarding those resources. Residents of off-grid communities take steps, including recharging aquifers, conserving watershed regions, and reducing water waste to maintain the reliability of their water supplies.

The cyclical aspect of water in the ecosystem is also much appreciated, which this practice fosters. Off-grid communities respect the delicate balance of the ecosystem and water availability throughout the year because they adapt their water collection tactics to the changing seasons.

Water collection from natural sources is crucial to off-grid living because it exemplifies the values of sustainability and harmony with the natural world. Individuals that make use of natural resources like water from rain, springs, wells, streams, and even fog are showing their resourcefulness, flexibility, and concern for the natural world. In addition to developing a profound connection with the natural world and its gifts, this information also allows off-grid communities to secure a key life-giving resource.

Harvesting Rainwater

Rainwater harvesting is a sustainable and environmentally friendly method of using rainwater for other purposes. It's a tried-and-true method for taking advantage of the existing water supply in the natural environment, and it's crucial for off-the-grid survival and water conservation.

The first step in rainwater harvesting is selecting an appropriate catchment area, such as a roof, gutter, or other impervious surface. When it rains on one of these surfaces, the water is directed into a collection system via downspouts and pipelines. Tanks, barrels, or cisterns collect and store the rainwater for later use.

The ease and versatility of rainwater harvesting is one of its main benefits. Those living off the grid can build rainwater gathering systems with common supplies and simple equipment. This convenience makes it an effective remedy for areas with inadequate or unreliable access to conventional water supplies.

Rainwater gathering encourages self-sufficiency by providing off-grid communities with a water supply that is not dependent on external sources or infrastructure. Individuals' reliance on already-stressed groundwater, rivers, and municipal water systems can be reduced by rainwater collection, mitigating the severity of the problem.

Rainwater harvesting promotes sustainability and environmental consciousness beyond its practical use. People who live off the grid can prevent soil erosion and the loss of topsoil by collecting rainwater to use later. This method also aids in groundwater recharging, which helps maintain the balance of the hydrologic cycle.

Rainwater has a wide variety of practical applications. Water unsuitable for human consumption can be used for cleaning, laundry, and watering plants and livestock. Rainwater, after going through the right processes of filtration and purification, can be used as a safe and reliable water source for off-grid communities.

In addition, the ethics of conservation and sustainable living are consistent with rainwater gathering. Off-grid residents strengthen their ties to the land and learn to take better care of water supplies by appreciating and putting them to good use.

Collecting rainwater for later use is a great example of how people and the natural world can work together for mutual benefit. It promotes environmental stewardship and lessens the ecological imprint while giving residents of off-grid settlements access to a steady water supply. Rainwater harvesting exemplifies the art of eco-friendly living by using the valuable gift of water, which is essential to all forms of life.

Effective Filtration and Purification Techniques

Proper filtration and purification techniques are essential to guarantee that water is safe and usable in off-grid survival scenarios. These methods are crucial for purifying and storing water harvested from natural sources like rain and surface water for human consumption.

The first step in purifying water is the filtration process. This process involves filtering out bigger particles and other physical contaminants from the water supply. Cloth filters are on the simpler end of the filtration spectrum, while sand and gravel filters are on the more intricate end. The basic idea is to filter water through a media that collects trash and silt so that the water that emerges is cleaner.

Because of the potential lack of access to contemporary filtration systems when living off the grid, the ability to improvise is a vital survival skill. Filters composed of clean scraps of fabric or clothing are good at trapping bigger dust and dirt particles. A container with alternating layers of sand and gravel can act like a natural filter, with the coarser layers capturing the largest particles and the finer ones collecting the tiniest impurities.

If there are any microorganisms or chemicals in the water after filtration, the next stage is purification. Off-grinders can choose from several efficient purifying processes, including:

Boiling

Water purification by boiling it in a pot over a fire is one of the oldest and most tried and true techniques. Pathogens can't survive in high temperatures. Therefore, the water is safe to drink. This approach, however, needs a heat source. Thus, it might only sometimes be applicable.

Chemicals

Water can be disinfected, and hazardous bacteria killed using chemicals like iodine or chlorine in a chemical purification process. Hikers and campers frequently opt for these purification pills or drops because of their convenience and portability.

UV Purification

Water purification by the sun's UV radiation is known as solar disinfection (SODIS). Leaving water in plastic bottles in the sun for several hours is an excellent way to eliminate most disease-causing organisms. This approach is both economical and sustainable.

Ceramic filters

The porous properties of ceramic filters allow for the efficient removal of germs and protozoa from water. They endure a long time, and they can be used repeatedly after washing them.

Filtration

Combining filtration and purification procedures is essential for effective water treatment in off-grid environments due to eliminating both physical and microbiological impurities. Off-grid residents can improve their health, happiness, and ability to live sustainably in peace with nature by selecting and applying these methods to purify water acquired from natural resources.

Building Irrigation Systems

To grow crops, care for gardens, and continue farming in locations with little or unpredictable water supplies, off-gridders must rely on irrigation systems, the construction of which is a key off-grid practice. Because they let people capture and control water for agricultural uses, these systems are essential to self-sufficiency and food security.

Understanding the land and water needs is the first step in constructing an irrigation system. Off-grid communities pay close attention to their surroundings, analyzing soil quality, slope, and water resources. They look at natural water flow patterns and investigate possible water suppliers for the irrigation system, including springs, wells, or rainwater catchment systems.

Surface and drip irrigation are the two most common varieties of irrigation systems.

With surface irrigation, water is flooded over fields or garden beds in a managed fashion. Ditching or digging channels allow water transported from a reservoir to the fields. The water trickles down the field, feeding the plants' roots as it seeps into the ground. Surface irrigation is a quick and cheap technique that works well in vast agricultural regions with abundant water.

Drip irrigation is a more accurate and water-efficient technique that uses a system of pipes, tubes, and emitters to supply water directly to the plant roots. This strategy reduces water waste while giving plants what they need to thrive, leading to fruitful harvests. Drip irrigation is ideal when water is scarce, or efficiency is a key issue.

When constructing surface irrigation systems, digging trenches or furrows and constructing embankments or berms to direct water flow are all possible. To prevent some regions from becoming waterlogged and to ensure equitable distribution, meticulous planning is required. Using swales or contour channels in conjunction with surface irrigation is an efficient water management method on hilly land because it helps retain water and prevents soil erosion.

Drip irrigation systems require pipes or tubes installed with emitters placed close to each plant. Drip lines can be installed at ground level or just below. Gravity-fed drip systems are ideal for off-grid communities because they require no additional power source. These systems pump water via pipes using pressure generated from water sources at a higher elevation.

Conserving water is one of the most important considerations when designing an irrigation system. To conserve water, off-grid communities plan their irrigation cycles and implement other water-saving measures. The system's longevity can be improved by collecting and utilizing rainfall or greywater from indoor plumbing.

The ability to cultivate land, nurture plant life, and promote self-sufficiency in food production is greatly enhanced by installing irrigation systems in off-grid dwellings. A stronger connection with nature and the land that nourishes them can be fostered by creating a thriving and sustainable agricultural ecosystem by off-grid residents through an awareness of the land's features, selecting appropriate irrigation systems, and implementing efficient water management strategies.

3. **If you haven't already done so, scan the QR code at the beginning of the book** and download THE BEST SURVIVAL DIY PROJECTS eBook + VIDEOS.

4. **Scan the QR code below and leave quick feedback on Amazon!**

SCAN ME

Book 3:

Generating Alternative Energy

Off-grid energy generation is a game-changer since it enables people to use renewable resources and cut their carbon footprint. Taking advantage of nature's wealth of renewable energy sources, this method exemplifies the values of sustainability and environmental responsibility.

Solar power is a significant contributor to the alternative energy sector. Solar panels harness the sun's energy and provide electricity to those who live off the grid. These panels absorb sunlight and convert it into a direct current (DC) electrical flow, typically placed on rooftops or in other exposed locations.

Off-grid communities use battery systems to store excess electricity produced during sunny days to make the most of their solar power. These batteries store the excess energy for use later, such as during overcast days or at night. People living off the grid benefit from this method because they no longer rely on the utility company for their electricity needs.

Many off-grid communities are beginning to utilize wind energy as an important alternative source. Locations with consistent wind flow can benefit from wind turbines, which transform the kinetic energy of the moving air into electricity. A wind turbine is a renewable energy source that uses the motion of the wind to power a generator.

Micro-hydro systems produce energy in areas with a high volume of running water. Like wind turbines, water turbines generate power by being spun by the flow of water in streams or small rivers. Micro-hydro systems are adaptable and effective, offering a steady and dependable supply of electricity.

Biomass energy has promise as a supplementary supply for those living off the grid. Combustion, gasification, and anaerobic digestion are all viable methods for transforming biomass such as wood, crop leftovers, and animal waste into usable bioenergy. Bioenergy is a renewable source of energy that may be used for things like heating, cooking, and producing electricity.

Furthermore, off-grid communities investigate geothermal energy, using the earth's natural heat to generate electricity and heat and cool structures. By tapping into underground reserves of hot water or steam, geothermal power plants can generate electricity by tapping into the earth's natural thermal energy source.

Creating alternative energy sources strengthens one's bond with the natural world and highlights the significance of long-term sustainability. People who live off the grid understand that their energy choices leave a little footprint on the planet and aid in the fight against climate change because of the renewable nature of these sources.

In conclusion, the ability to generate alternative energy while living off-grid is a powerful symbol of creativity and resourcefulness. Individuals can break free from the shackles of traditional energy sources and choose a lifestyle that is in harmony with the cycles of nature and beneficial to the earth by taking advantage of renewable energy sources like the sun, wind, water, biomass, and geothermal heat. This effort to become energy independent indicates a serious dedication to a future in which people can live in peace with the planet and its natural resources.

Harnessing Solar Power for Electricity

Using the sun's rays to produce electricity is a sustainable and revolutionary approach that allows people to produce clean, renewable energy. Solar panels, also known as photovoltaic (PV), transform solar energy into usable electricity.

Solar cells, primarily comprised of semiconductor materials like silicon, are assembled into solar panels. When exposed to sunlight, these cells generate an electric current, which excites electrons inside the cells. The electricity is then wired to a solar converter, which transforms the DC into the alternating current (AC) used by most homes and appliances today.

Solar panels in off-grid villages are usually positioned to get the most sunshine possible. Common places to find solar panels are on the roofs of buildings, in open fields, or at solar farms. The panels can be angled and positioned to maximize solar collection at any time of day or year.

Solar energy generation has the potential to grow as the demand for electricity rises. People living off the grid can get their feet wet with a modest solar array and scale up as their power needs increase. Individuals can adjust their solar power systems' size, cost, and other aspects to meet their needs.

Off-grid communities use battery storage devices to provide continuous power, even during low sunlight or at night. Batteries operate as reservoirs for energy, storing excess electricity generated during sunny hours. When the sun isn't shining or energy demand is higher than solar generating, the stored electricity is used to keep the lights on.

In solar power systems, efficient energy management is crucial. Off-grinders frequently use charge controllers to prevent the batteries from being overcharged or discharged. Energy production and consumption can be tracked using monitoring devices, allowing for more efficient use of resources and less environmental impact.

Using solar energy to generate electricity is a game-changer for self-sufficiency and environmental friendliness. By harnessing the sun's renewable energy instead of traditional fossil fuels, off-grid communities help minimize harmful emissions and protect the environment.

In addition to being a low-cost and low-maintenance option for off-grid electricity generation, solar power systems require very little regular maintenance. Solar panels are an excellent long-term investment because they may keep churning out electricity for decades after they've been installed.

In conclusion, using solar energy to generate electricity is a game-changing step toward a more sustainable and environmentally friendly energy future. Off-grid communities harness solar power to generate electricity and lessen their environmental footprint. Taking control of one's energy source this way encourages a stronger bond with the natural world and a determination to create a more sustainable society.

Building DIY Wind Turbines for Energy Generation

Individuals can harness wind power and generate clean, renewable electricity by building their own Do-It-Yourself (DIY) wind turbines, a method that is both empowering and sustainable. Off-grid communities can achieve energy independence at little cost by constructing their DIY wind turbines using commonplace materials.

DIY wind turbine construction starts with a well-thought-out plan and detailed blueprints. Those living off the grid must determine their energy requirements and the potential of the local wind resources. Information on wind speed and direction is essential for siting and sizing turbines. This assessment can be aided by online wind resource maps or wind speed data from nearby weather stations.

A do-it-yourself wind turbine consists mostly of the following:

The wind's kinetic energy is converted into rotational motion by the blades. Make your blade from anything from wood to PVC pipes to metal sheets. They are meticulously crafted for maximum effectiveness and efficiency.

The blades' rotational motion is transformed into electrical energy by the generator. Permanent magnet alternators (PMAs) are commonly used as generators in do-it-yourself (DIY) wind turbines in off-grid communities because they are inexpensive, widely available, and simple to assemble.

The wind turbine is supported by a tower, which elevates the device to an optimal height for harvesting wind energy. Towers for home-built wind turbines can be made of steel, wood, or other solid materials.

The wind turbine's tail and yaw mechanism allows it to continuously rotate and face the wind, maximizing its energy harvesting potential.

The do-it-yourself wind turbine calls for both mechanical and electrical know-how to construct. Off-grid communities follow precise guidance and instructions commonly available online or in DIY renewable energy publications to ensure their turbines' safe and effective building.

The next step in installing a do-it-yourself wind turbine is to mount it on the selected tower in a spot with plenty of wind. During the installation process, we pay close attention to safety measures to forestall mishaps and guarantee the integrity of the building.

Excess energy produced by home-built wind turbines during windy seasons can be stored in battery storage devices. Then, when the wind isn't blowing as strongly, or it's nighttime, people living off the grid can use this stored energy to keep their lights on.

DIY wind turbines need regular inspections and maintenance to run safely and efficiently. Checking the blades, generator, tower, and other parts regularly helps find problems early and keeps the wind turbine running smoothly.

In conclusion, off-grid communities can benefit greatly from and be empowered by the initiative of erecting their wind turbines for energy generation. By converting wind energy into a usable form, people can lessen their environmental impact, aid in conservation efforts, and strengthen their connection to the natural world around them. Off-grid residents can take control of their energy destiny by building their DIY wind turbines, exemplifying the pioneering and independent spirit.

5. **If you haven't already done so, scan the QR code at the beginning of the book** and download THE BEST SURVIVAL DIY PROJECTS eBook + VIDEOS.

6. **Scan the QR code below and leave quick feedback on Amazon!**

SCAN ME

Book 4:

Sustainable Hunting and Fishing Practices

Responsible resource management is an art form, and sustainable hunting and fishing are prime examples of this in the world of off-the-grid life. The fragile balance of the planet's ecosystems can only be maintained if human needs and conservation work in tandem.

Sustainable hunting in off-the-grid societies is achieved by applying age-old practices and knowledge passed down through the ages. They value and appreciate wildlife and regard hunting as necessary for securing food and resources. The practice of selective hunting, in which only specific species members are killed to maintain stable reproductive populations, has gained prominence.

The ethics of hunting highlight the significance of swift and humane kills. People living off the grid know that treating animals with dignity and respect is essential to the natural order of things. They learn to hunt like their forefathers did, becoming adept gatherers of food and protectors of the natural world.

Off-grid communities' fishing methods are consistent with sustainability principles because of their awareness of the value of a healthy aquatic habitat. Their practice of catch-and-release exemplifies their dedication to protecting fish populations while enjoying the sport of fishing. They use barbless hooks and non-toxic fishing gear to conserve fish populations and valuable aquatic ecosystems.

Off-grid residents know the value of protecting endangered species and conserving natural diversity, so they make it a point to abide by local fishing restrictions and avoid certain locations. They want to work with local conservation agencies and indigenous tribes to ensure their methods align with sustainable wildlife management efforts.

The philosophy of sustainable resource harvesting extends beyond traditional methods of gathering food and medicine, including hunting and fishing. Traditional knowledge of native plants and their uses is highly valued in off-grid communities. They forage carefully not to harm the ecosystem or endangered species without which they could not survive.

Off-grid communities are models of sustainability because they look beyond their needs to those of future generations. They consider themselves stewards of the land and water that provide for them, responsible for maintaining their natural beauty and functionality. Nature's abundance is praised, and sustainable practices for handling the planet's resources have become the norm.

Off-the-grid communities that employ sustainable hunting and fishing methods demonstrate the mutual benefits of coexisting with nature. Wildlife and fish populations benefit from these approaches because they combine traditional knowledge with current conservation concepts. By practicing responsible hunting, fishing, and foraging, off-the-grid communities can enjoy the benefits of the wilderness while preserving it for future generations.

Hunting

Hunting, the practice of actively seeking out and killing wild animals for food, ritual, or sport, has a long and significant history in human culture. Humans' ability to hunt is evidence of our deep evolutionary roots in the natural world and our adaptability to life in the wild.

Hunting has been essential to human existence since our earliest settlements, giving us food and materials. To ensure a successful hunt, our ancestors perfected their talents at reading the land and the behavior of animals. They could survive in the wild with only the most basic tools and weapons, and they gladly accepted their place as predators in the web of life.

Hunting has traditionally been honored for its spiritual and cultural value. Many indigenous groups' customs, rituals, and beliefs revolve around hunting. It's a spiritual deed that symbolizes the unity of all life and the acceptance of the inevitable passage from this world to the next.

Hunting as we know it now has adapted to include new technologies, but its core principles have remained the same. Some people see hunting as a method to provide for themselves and maintain a healthy relationship with the land. For others, it is a chance to create lasting memories with loved ones via shared adventure.

However, there are ethical and moral questions raised by hunting. Ethical hunting is more important than ever because of threats to the environment and the fragile equilibrium of ecosystems. Hunters in off-the-grid areas know the significance of maintaining healthy and abundant animal populations.

Hunters that practice ethical hunting put the welfare of the animals they pursue first. Today's Hunters strive for swift and humane kills because they understand the weight of the decision to kill an animal for food. They avoid damaging the environment and actively work to maintain natural environments.

Hunting is more than just a means to an end; it's an intricate and comprehensive activity in its own right. It sums up our deep relationships with nature, rich history, and environmental stewardship obligations. Hunting, whether for food, ritual, or sport, represents our intrinsic capacity to navigate the wild and cohabit with the natural environment, paying respect to the intricate dance of life unfolding since the beginning of time.

Freshwater Fishing

Fishing in freshwater environments, such as rivers, lakes, ponds, and streams, is known as fishing. Many people worldwide like doing this as a hobby and a way to supplement their diet. Fishing in freshwater is one of the oldest practices in human history, extending back thousands of years as a means of subsistence.

People use rods, lines, hooks, and bait or lures to catch fish in freshwater. You'll need a flexible fishing rod constructed of diverse materials like fiberglass or carbon fiber to throw the line and reel in the catch. The hook, bait, or lure is at the end of the fishing line, which is tied to the fishing rod.

Numerous freshwater fish species exist, each adapted to a unique climate and environmental conditions. Trout, bass, catfish, perch, pike, and carp are just a few examples of common freshwater fish. Different fishing methods and bait selections are needed to catch each species successfully.

There's a wide range of emotions you might experience while freshwater fishing, from peaceful moments of seclusion in tranquil lakes to the adrenaline rush of fighting powerful fish in swift rivers. It's a great way to relax, spend time outside, and appreciate the splendor of our planet's pristine freshwater environments.

Freshwater fishing is regulated in many areas through fishing licenses and seasons to guarantee sustainable practices and safeguard fish populations. Catch-and-release fishing is a common conservation strategy because it allows anglers to experience the thrill of fishing while also helping protect fish populations by releasing them back into the water unharmed.

The conservation and study of the natural world are two additional benefits of freshwater fishing. This information is invaluable for researchers examining fish populations, water quality, and aquatic ecosystems. This information aids our knowledge of freshwater biodiversity and guides our preservation efforts.

Ethical considerations are crucial in freshwater fishing, as in hunting or fishing. Conscient fishermen adhere to catch restrictions and other rules to maintain healthy freshwater ecosystems and preserve fish populations. They also take precautions to ensure the survival of fish they catch and release to reduce their impact on aquatic ecosystems.

Freshwater fishing is a tradition enjoyed by people of all ages and cultures for many years. It helps people connect with the environment, provides opportunities for recreation and learning, and aids in studying and protecting freshwater ecosystems. Freshwater fishing celebrates the richness and variety of the world's freshwater ecosystems, whether for sport, subsistence, or scientific inquiry.

Sea Fishing

In the open waters of oceans, seas, and coastal regions, fishermen cast their lines in search of fish and other marine organisms. Millions of people worldwide participate in this time-honored tradition because of the fascinating and varied fishing opportunities presented by the ocean's vastness.

To overcome the problems of the ever-changing marine environment, fishermen need specific gear and methods. To endure the corrosive effects of saltwater and the strength of larger and stronger fish species, sea fishing rods and reels tend to be more robust and durable than their freshwater counterparts.

There are numerous sea fishing approaches, each suited to a particular set of circumstances. Casting lines from the shore or piers is known as "shore fishing," while fishing from a boat or ship takes anglers to deeper waters. When fishing for large, powerful game fish, deep-sea fishing requires venturing even further from shore.

From tiny coastal fish to massive predators like tuna, marlin, and swordfish, a tremendous variety of marine species is available for sea fishing. Anglers may catch many different fish species, each requiring unique skills and bait.

By going out to sea to fish, you may experience the raw force and beauty of the ocean while also discovering beautiful coastal vistas. For many people living along the world's coasts, fishing is a way to provide for their families and make a living.

Sea fishing is no different than any other type of fishing in that it requires careful and long-term planning. Catch limits, fishing rules, and closed seasons are commonly implemented to prevent overfishing and preserve marine ecosystems' delicate biological balance. For the sake of marine conservation, responsible anglers employ catch-and-release methods that allow released fish to thrive.

Fishing in the ocean also helps with marine conservation and research. Anglers and scientists work together to collect important information for conserving and managing marine ecosystems and fish populations.

Sea fishing is a fascinating and satisfying activity since it allows people to connect with nature while also providing them with the excitement of catching a wide variety of marine animals. It helps people feel more connected to the ocean and its inhabitants and contributes to environmental protection and wise resource management. Whether for sport, subsistence, or scientific inquiry, fishing on the open sea celebrates the sea's astonishing diversity of life.

7. **If you haven't already done so, scan the QR code at the beginning of the book** and download THE BEST SURVIVAL DIY PROJECTS eBook + VIDEOS.

8. **Scan the QR code below and leave quick feedback on Amazon!**

SCAN ME

Book 5:

Food Production and Conservation

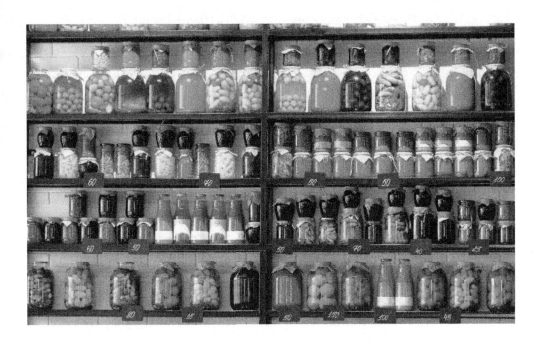

Sustainable agriculture and conservation work hand in hand to protect both human health and the delicate balance of natural systems.

"food production" refers to the entire chain of operations, from planting seeds to eating the final result. Conventional methods in modern agriculture have typically prioritized productivity and yields over other factors, leading to heavy usage of chemical fertilizers, pesticides, and widespread monoculture. However, such actions often have unintended negative consequences, such as reduced soil fertility, the contamination of water sources, and the loss of biodiversity.

On the other hand, sustainable food production prioritizes conserving natural resources and minimizing the impact on the surrounding ecosystem. Sustainable farming methods that emphasize soil health, biodiversity, and natural ecosystem services include organic farming, permaculture, and agroecology. Crop rotation, composting, intercropping, and integrated pest control are common practices in sustainable agriculture that help farmers use less synthetic chemicals while bolstering ecological resilience.

On the other hand, conservation is concerned with the safekeeping of ecosystems and various forms of flora and fauna. Preserving ecosystems and biodiversity includes saving endangered species and preventing their extinction. Ecosystems, the basis of food production and global well-being, can only survive long-term if conservation efforts are successful.

Protected areas, animal corridors, and marine sanctuaries are all conservation measures that can be used in food production. For land and sea creatures alike, these protected zones are essential for survival and fulfilling their ecological responsibilities.

There is a recursive relationship between conservation efforts and agricultural output. Sustainable agriculture aids preservation efforts by reducing negative environmental effects and bolstering biodiverse ecosystems. In turn, conservation activities guarantee the survival of various habitats, which often serve as the basis for long-term, environmentally-friendly farming, and food production.

The protection of pollinators is an excellent illustration of this connection. Pollinators like bees and butterflies are essential to agriculture because they spread pollen from flower to flower. Pollinator populations, bolstered by conservation initiatives that protect habitats and increase biodiversity, boost crop yields, which benefits food production.

The delicate dance that keeps life on Earth going comprises food production and conservation. Protecting the ecosystems that sustain agriculture is a key component of sustainable food production techniques, encouraging ecological balance and resource stewardship. Individuals and communities can help ensure future food security and environmental health by adopting both approaches.

Cultivating Off-Grid Gardens

Growing your food, getting in touch with nature, and encouraging self-sufficiency in distant and off-grid living conditions are all made possible by cultivating off-grid gardens. Off-the-grid gardens are oases of plenty in the desert, producing healthy food while decreasing reliance on commercial farms.

Planning and site selection are the first steps in growing an off-grid garden. Space in off-grid settlements is evaluated based on criteria like access to natural resources like water and sunlight. They frequently use permaculture techniques, balancing the garden with its natural environment to ensure its continued health.

Gardeners that cultivate their crops away from the grid value soil health and instead employ organic and regenerative farming methods. Natural fertilizers and compost add to the soil's nutrient content, making it ideal for plant growth. Off-the-grid gardens are like little ecosystems unto themselves.

Crops are selected considering the time of year, weather patterns, and individual nutritional preferences. A healthy and well-rounded diet can be maintained through an off-the-grid gardener's cultivation of various edible and medicinal plants. Open-pollinated and heirloom seeds are preferred because they are more hardy and help maintain plant diversity.

Irrigating the garden using collected rainfall and recycled graywater is common in off-the-grid communities. Mulching and drip irrigation are two examples of water-saving practices used to reduce unnecessary water use and stabilize the water supply.

Off-the-grid gardeners put forth a lot of time and effort because they value their relationship with the Earth. Those who cultivate off the grid do it with great care, paying close attention to the details of nature and developing a rich awareness of the ecology in which they live.

Off-grid gardens have many uses beyond just feeding people. They help maintain a healthy ecosystem by providing homes for pollinators, migratory birds, and other species. Gardens aid in soil and water conservation and operate as carbon sinks, removing CO_2 from the air.

Off-grid gardens help people meet their basic needs and improve their quality of life. Feelings of purpose, accomplishment, and fulfillment can be gained from gardening as one watches their efforts bear fruit.

Ultimately, off-grid gardening symbolizes peace with the natural world and gratitude for Earth's rich blessings. It exemplifies the values of independence, ingenuity, and environmental stewardship, allowing off-the-grid communities to create a flourishing garden paradise amid the wilderness and set out on a path toward a life of sustainable harmony with the natural world.

Foraging for Wild Edibles

The practice of foraging refers to the skill of discovering and acquiring food sources in the outdoors. Identifying and using plants locally was crucial to the survival of our ancestors and so had deep historical roots in human culture. Foraging has seen a renaissance in the modern era as people seek new ways to strengthen their ties to the natural world, adopt eco-friendly lifestyles, and rediscover wild foods' deliciousness and health advantages.

Foragers venture into various environments, from rural to urban, to find and gather wild foods. The term "wild edibles" refers to a wide variety of plants that humans can consume, such as edible leaves, flowers, fruits, nuts, seeds, and mushrooms. Fiddlehead ferns, wild garlic, and dandelion greens are some of the most well-known examples.

Identifying plants is a crucial part of foraging. Foragers need to be familiar with the local flora to know which plants are safe and poisonous to eat. If you want to stay safe and prevent becoming sick from eating something hazardous, you need to be able to identify it correctly.

The long-term health of wild plant populations depends on responsible foragers. Foragers practice sustainable harvesting practices, taking only what they need while leaving the plant with enough to sustain its growth and reproduction. They also don't take any chances by harvesting endangered animals either.

The abundance of wild edibles fluctuates with the seasons, making foraging a dynamic and seasonal pursuit. Depending on the season, you can enjoy various plant flavors and nutrients. Respecting the natural cycles of plants and adjusting their foraging methods accordingly, foragers live in harmony with the natural world.

Foraging has many advantages beyond just the food it may provide. Some species of wild delicacies have higher quantities of vitamins, minerals, and antioxidants than cultivated crops, and they often have distinctive flavors. A sense of appreciation and reverence for nature's gifts can also be developed via foraging.

Foraging can bring people together, allowing for the exchange of stories and tips. To share knowledge and experience, forager groups may hold walks, workshops, or other types of gatherings.

Foraging can be a wonderful way to learn about nature and expand one's horizons, but it's important to do so safely and responsibly. Cleaning and preparing wild foods properly is essential for food safety and removing pollutants.

Exploring the outdoors for food is a time-honored tradition that strengthens ties to the earth and its bounty. It exemplifies the core principles of eco-friendly lifestyles by teaching people to value their natural surroundings and the bounty nature offers. Foragers travel in search of new knowledge and gastronomic experiences, enjoying the tastes of nature without negatively impacting the planet.

Food Preservation Techniques

Various techniques have been used for ages to preserve food, making it possible to eat well even in times of scarcity and saving the harvest for later use. Reducing food waste, increasing food security, and preserving the nutritional content of preserved foods are all important goals shared by off-grid communities and modern nations.

Drying or dehydrating food is one of the earliest and most used methods of food preservation. Dehydrating fruits, vegetables, and meats prevents the growth of spoilage germs, greatly increasing their storage life. Sun-drying, air-drying, and using contemporary machines like dehydrators are all viable options for drying.

Canning is another common way of preserving food, which entails sealing food in airtight containers and heating it to kill bacteria. The food is kept fresh and safe from spoilage for extended periods thanks to the vacuum seal created by this method. You may find canned fruits, vegetables, and meats in almost any supermarket worldwide.

Food's nutritional content and flavor can be improved through fermentation, a time-honored preservation method. Sugars are broken down by microbes like bacteria and yeast, producing acids or alcohol, which is toxic to spoilage germs. Pickles, kimchi, yogurt, and sauerkraut are all fermented foods.

To prevent spoilage due to bacterial growth, salt is used in the processes of salting and curing. Examples of foods that go through this procedure include bacon and ham. Salting is often done with smoking to increase the longevity and depth of flavor.

By bringing food to temperatures below freezing, we can prevent spoilage caused by microorganisms and enzymatic processes. Foods' texture, flavor, and nutritional value are all maintained by this process. You can get frozen meats, veggies, and fruits in grocery stores and kitchen freezers everywhere.

Vacuum sealing and refrigeration are only two examples of how food can be preserved with current technology. By removing the air from the package, vacuum sealing protects food from going bad or getting freezer burned. Perishable goods can be stored in a refrigerator longer without losing their freshness or safety.

The act of preserving food has multiple purposes, including the maintenance of cultural traditions and the perpetuation of culinary history. Communities have a sense of continuity and identity due to the many traditional recipes and methods passed down through the years.

The ability of humans to preserve nature's bounty through food preservation methods is a monument to their ingenuity and resourcefulness. Methods as varied as drying and freezing have been used for centuries to preserve the fruits of the crop for consumption at any time of the year. Preserving food is an important part of eco-friendly lifestyles since it helps cut down on food waste, improves food security, and honors the wide range of tastes and cuisines that make up our collective history.

9. **If you haven't already done so, scan the QR code at the beginning of the book** and download THE BEST SURVIVAL DIY PROJECTS eBook + VIDEOS.

10. **Scan the QR code below and leave quick feedback on Amazon!**

SCAN ME

Book 6:

Crafting Tools and Equipment

Making useful and necessary goods by hand utilizing a wide range of materials and time-honored methods is what is meant by "crafting tools and equipment." Self-sufficiency and the ability to meet one's requirements are vital in any setting, but they are crucial in off-the-grid communities.

Having a thorough familiarity with the local resources is the first step in making tools and equipment. Resources such as wood, metal, textiles, and others that can be turned into useful goods are identified and harvested by people living off the grid. They learn to make new uses for old things, which helps them save money and use resources better.

Because wood is so common in off-the-grid areas, woodworking is a crucial craft skill. Wood is shaped into everything from cooking utensils and storage containers to furniture and building materials by off-grid residents using hand tools, including saws, axes, chisels, and knives.

The ability to work with metals such as iron, steel, and copper makes metalworking a valuable skill. Knives, farming implements, and repair tools may be made out of scrap metal by members of off-grid communities using methods like forging, welding, or soldering.

Tools and equipment production also makes extensive use of weaving and textiles. Natural fibers, such as those derived from plants or animals, must be processed and woven into the fabric before they can be used to make things like clothing, blankets, and other textiles by those living off the grid.

Off-the-grid societies must be resourceful and inventive in their crafts since they must modify their products to fit their unique circumstances. They practice self-sufficiency and upcycling by repurposing unwanted materials to lessen their reliance on imported commodities.

In addition to serving a practical purpose, the tools and equipment we make reflect our heritage and showcase our skills. Building tools that complement the environment and the problems it presents encourages a more intimate relationship with the land and its resources.

Making one's tools and equipment symbolizes the ingenuity and independence that enable off-the-grid communities to prosper. It honors the resourcefulness of individuals who find ways to make do with what they have to meet their daily requirements and contribute to their communities. Crafting these items improves the quality of life for those who choose to live without grid power and strengthens their sense of cultural identity and connection to the natural world.

Primitive Technologies for Off-Grid Living

Primitive technologies for off-grid life are the age-old, culturally-specific approaches to providing for one's basic needs in undeveloped or wild areas. These methods were developed long before the advent of machines and relied instead on primitive implements, abundant materials, and inventive humans to fulfill basic requirements.

Fire is a crucial element in the development of many early tools. The capacity to make and manage fire is essential for survival, as it can be used for food preparation and heating and as a deterrent to predators and insects. Fire-making methods such as friction fire, flint and steel, and bow drills are well-known and used in off-grid communities.

The ability to build a shelter is another crucial rudimentary skill. People living off the grid typically construct crude but functional homes from materials like twigs, leaves, and animal skins. Lean-tos, rubble huts, and wattle-and-daub construction are all frequently used methods.

The ability to obtain and purify water is crucial for off-the-grid survival. Safe drinking water can be obtained using primitive technologies like digging wells, collecting rainwater, and constructing basic filtration systems from sand and charcoal.

Food gathering by foraging and hunting dates back thousands of years. Communities that don't have access to the grid often rely on their members' familiarity with edible wild plants and therapeutic herbs. Bows and arrows, spears, and traps are used for hunting and fishing, much as they were thousands of years ago.

Weaving and basketry are essential for storing containers, textiles, and other useful goods. Those living off the grid often make baskets, mats, and textiles from the plants and animals they gather.

Primitive pottery was essential for preserving and preparing food. Communities without reliable access to the power grid often make their pottery by hand or with simple tools out of clay and then fire it in open flames or pit kilns.

Off-the-grinders can tie down their homes, make traps, and build their tools and equipment using natural cordage and ropes from plant fibers.

The stars, the sun, and familiar landmarks can all be used for basic navigation when you're out in the woods.

Stones and flint are used in stonework and flint knapping to create various tools.

These archaic methods demonstrate the human species' robustness, inventiveness, and versatility in off-the-grid settings. They indicate the people's closeness to the land and capacity to use its resources to satisfy basic wants. While contemporary technology has made many things easier, those who seek self-sufficiency and a deeper connection to the natural world might benefit from learning and practicing ancient methods.

Essential Handmade Tools and Utensils

Items manufactured by hand using traditional processes and materials are essential handmade tools and utensils. These tools and utensils are essential for off-grid life and self-sufficiency in areas with limited or prohibitive access to manufactured items. Handmade tools and utensils exemplify the ideals of resourcefulness, sustainability, and cultural heritage, demonstrating off-grid populations' inventiveness in meeting their basic requirements.

Knives: Knives are multipurpose tools that are used for cooking, hunting, crafts, and a variety of daily duties. Handcrafted knives are created from metals such as steel or recycled materials, and their style and shape are personalized to the individual's specific demands and preferences.

Hand-carved wooden spoons, spatulas, and ladles are indispensable for cooking and food preparation. They are made of wood, often derived from sustainably managed forests, and are fashioned to be useful and visually beautiful.

In clay pottery, handmade clay pots and vessels are used for cooking, food storage, and water containers. They are made by hand or with simple equipment and burnt in open fires or kilns, providing a traditional and environmentally friendly alternative to modern cookware.

Woven Baskets: Handwoven baskets are multifunctional containers for gathering, storing, and transporting objects. They are constructed from plant fibers such as reeds or grasses and reflect the community's traditional weaving traditions.

Hand-carved wooden bowls and containers are used for serving food, holding objects, and crafts hobbies. They are molded and smoothed by hand, displaying the craftsperson's talent and artistry.

Cordage and Ropes: Handmade cordage and ropes are composed of natural fibers such as plant or animal fibers. They are utilized in numerous off-grid activities for tying buildings, making traps, and fastening objects.

Hand-forged Tools: Blacksmithing processes create hand-forged tools such as axes, hammers, and chisels. They are strong and long-lasting, making them excellent for various operations such as woodworking, building, and metalworking.

Weaving and Textiles: Handwoven fabrics and textiles are made from plant or animal fibers and are used to make clothing, blankets, and other necessities.

Flint and Steel Fire Starter: Handcrafted flint and steel fire starters are dependable for lighting fires in off-grid environments. They are based on traditional fire-making skills passed down through centuries.

Handmade leather items like belts, pouches, and sheaths provide long-lasting and efficient alternatives for carrying and organizing tools and personal possessions.

Handmade tools and utensils demonstrate off-grid populations' resourcefulness and craftsmanship. Each piece reflects a link to the land, cultural legacy, and time-honed abilities. In a world that often values mass-produced items, these handcrafted tools and utensils exemplify self-sufficiency and the wisdom of generations past.

11. **If you haven't already done so, scan the QR code at the beginning of the book** and download THE BEST SURVIVAL DIY PROJECTS eBook + VIDEOS.

12. **Scan the QR code below and leave quick feedback on Amazon!**

SCAN ME

Book 7:

Herbal Medicine and Natural Remedies

"herbal medicine" and "natural remedies" describe using plants and plant-derived chemicals for therapeutic purposes. Humans have used this treatment method for eons, and it is an integral part of many different cultures' approaches to healthcare today.

Herbal medicine is practiced on the assumption that plant healing properties can supplement the body's innate capacity to repair and restore itself. Leaves, petals, roots, and bark are only some plant parts used for their therapeutic value. Teas, tinctures, poultices, salves, capsules, and capsules are all viable delivery systems for these medicinal substances.

Individualization, or adapting treatment to each patient's unique condition, is a central tenet of herbal medicine. Herbalists look at the whole person, not just the physical symptoms, to choose the best course of treatment.

Natural and herbal medicines treat a wide variety of illnesses. Some plants offer pain-relieving and inflammation-calming qualities thanks to their anti-inflammatory characteristics. Some are effective in treating infections because of their antiseptic and antibacterial properties. Herbal treatments are widely utilized for various health benefits, including immune system support, digestion aid, sleep improvement, stress mitigation, and anxiety reduction.

Herbal medicine is a technique with profound roots in the traditional healing modalities of many different cultures and indigenous communities, and its knowledge is often passed down through the years. Herbal medicine has become an important part of the healthcare system in many areas of the world, particularly in regions where conventional medical care is scarce.

There has been a recent upsurge of interest in Western nations in herbal therapy and other alternative therapies. More and more people are turning away from conventional medicine in favor of alternative and complementary therapies to improve their health and well-being.

But it's important to take caution while using herbal medication and get advice from knowledgeable herbalists or doctors. Some herbs may have drug interactions or contraindications when used with other treatments, even though many are perfectly safe and effective. Effective and safe use requires careful attention to dosing and preparation.

Using herbs and other natural medicines is a worthwhile and tried therapy method. They are a tribute to the effectiveness of natural remedies and time-tested care methods. Herbal medicine, whether used alone or in conjunction with conventional medicine, is a powerful symbol of humanity's deep bond with the natural world and the abundance of natural remedies available.

Utilizing Medicinal Plants for Health and Healing

Regarding health and healing, medicinal plants aid in prevention, treatment, and the body's healing mechanisms. Recognizing nature's therapeutic potential and the wealth of medicinal chemicals contained in various plant species is a practice with deep roots in traditional medicine systems worldwide.

The theory behind the use of medicinal plants is that these substances exist in plants and can benefit the body's physiology. These molecules may exert beneficial effects, such as those of anti-inflammatories, antimicrobials, analgesics, and antioxidants.

Common ailments like colds, coughs, and stomach difficulties can all be treated with herbal medication, as can chronic conditions like arthritis, diabetes, and anxiety. Some people utilize medicinal herbs to help them sleep better, feel less stressed, and boost their immune systems.

Depending on the plant and the ailment, many routes of administration may be used for herbal treatments. Here are some often-used techniques:

Herbal teas, often infusions, are prepared by steeping dried or fresh plant material in hot water. Many people use this method because it's easy and tastes good when using medicinal plants.

Alcohol or glycerin extracts the active components from medicinal plant material, creating a tincture. Herbal medication in the form of tinctures is more potent and may be stored for longer.

Herbal capsules are made from finely powdered dried herbs, then capsuled for easy administration.

Infused oils, salves, and poultices are applied topically to treat skin issues, muscle pain, and wounds.

Herbal baths are a popular way to relax and treat skin problems, and they can be made with either dried or fresh herbs.

Aromatherapy involves inhaling or topical administering essential oils produced from plants used for therapeutic purposes.

Even while medicinal plants can be helpful companions in promoting health and healing, they should be used with understanding and caution. It is best to seek the advice of a qualified herbalist or medical expert to ensure safe and effective plant selection, dosing, and avoidance of drug interactions.

In addition, protecting plant populations and maintaining biodiversity relies heavily on sustainable and ethical harvesting practices. With more and more people turning to herbal remedies, we must spread awareness about the importance of sustainable herbalism.

Using plants for healing and wellness acknowledges the value of experience-based knowledge and the bond between humans and the natural world. This treatment method promotes overall health and wellness by considering the whole person rather than just their physical symptoms. Individuals can take a more holistic and individualized approach to their health journey when the medicinal power of plants is incorporated into healthcare.

Preparing Natural First Aid Supplies

Preparing natural first aid supplies entails putting together a collection of medicinal plants, herbal treatments, and natural compounds that can be used to treat common injuries, illnesses, and emergencies. These products supplement or replace traditional first aid kits by utilizing nature's healing power to provide relief and assistance in times of need.

Herbal Infused Oils: To extract the curative properties of medicinal herbs, infused oils are created by steeping them in carrier oils such as olive or coconut oil. Massage, topical treatments, and wound care are all possibilities.

Herbal salves and balms blend infused oils with beeswax or other natural waxes. They provide a portable and handy method of applying herbal medicines to the skin for wound healing, burns, and irritations.

Tinctures are concentrated herbal extracts created by soaking herbs in alcohol or glycerin. They give a powerful and long-lasting herbal medication that can be used internally and externally.

Herbal Teas: Teas made from dried or fresh medicinal herbs can treat various health ailments, including digestive disorders, respiratory problems, and stress alleviation.

Aloe vera gel is a natural treatment for burns, sunburns, and skin irritations. It provides calming and therapeutic effects that relieve discomfort and aid skin repair.

Activated charcoal is a natural chemical known for absorbing toxins and poisons. It can be used to treat poisoning or upset stomach, and indigestion.

Essential oils are extracted from fragrant herbs and have a variety of medicinal qualities. Some essential oils, such as lavender and tea tree oil, have antibacterial and calming properties that make them suitable for first aid.

Arnica cream is a natural treatment for bruises, sprains, and muscle pain. Topically applied arnica cream can help to reduce inflammation and facilitate healing.

Epsom Salt Baths: Epsom salt baths can help relieve muscle aches and pains while promoting relaxation.

Honey: Raw honey has natural antibacterial qualities and can be used as a wound care topical treatment.

It is critical to have a basic awareness of each medicine's qualities and acceptable usage while making natural first aid supplies. Consulting with a skilled herbalist or healthcare practitioner can help you choose and use the best medicines for your condition.

Natural first aid items can be utilized in various scenarios, including minor injuries, burns, skin irritations, respiratory difficulties, and stress alleviation. They provide a more holistic and natural approach to resolving health difficulties, reflecting humans' fundamental connection with the natural world's healing potential.

1. **If you haven't already done so, scan the QR code at the beginning of the book** and download THE BEST SURVIVAL DIY PROJECTS eBook + VIDEOS.

2. **Scan the QR code below and leave quick feedback on Amazon!**

SCAN ME

Book 8:

Personal Protection and Security

When people talk about "personal protection and security off the grid," they're referring to the steps they take to safeguard themselves and their possessions when they're far from civilization's protection and support systems. Living off the grid comes with its own difficulties, making personal safety much more important.

Protecting oneself from physical harm and potential risks in the outdoors typically necessitates acquiring self-defense and survival skills by those living off the grid. Learning self-defense, wilderness survival skills, and using weapons effectively is crucial when venturing into uncharted territories.

Building a safe and sturdy home is a top consideration for those who live independently from the power grid. Reinforced doors and windows are only two security measures that can help keep out burglars and wild animals, but there are many more.

Gun Ownership: Residents of some off-the-grid areas prefer to arm themselves with firearms to deter predators and criminals. The ownership of a firearm requires training, secure storage, and compliance with all applicable laws and regulations.

Nonetheless, people who live off the grid keep in touch with their neighbors and form networks to help one another out in times of crisis. Keeping in touch allows for rapidly disseminating information in an emergency and facilitates the timely mitigation of hazards.

Off-grid communities frequently collaborate to increase their safety. Neighborhood watch programs, emergency response plans, and dissemination of information about suspicious activity enhance the communal feeling of safety.

Knowledge of the Terrain and Surrounding Dangers Being familiar with the surrounding terrain, fauna, and potential dangers is crucial to ensuring one's safety. Individuals can better respond to natural disasters like wildfires and floods if they know the local climate, weather patterns, and hazards.

Maintaining a constant and reliable food and water supply is crucial to safety when living off the grid. Reducing reliance on external resources and protecting against shortages, gardening, and agriculture allow people to grow food and collect and purify water.

Cybersecurity and digital privacy are still important considerations for those living off the grid. Identity theft and other forms of data breach can be avoided if digital assets, sensitive data, and communication channels are secure.

Setting Boundaries: Life off the grid can involve long periods of seclusion and the possibility of chance contact with strangers. Establishing and enforcing firm limits is the best way to protect one's privacy and safety.

Off-Grid Survival Requires a Higher Level of Emergency Preparation. It is important for people to be prepared for emergencies and know how to provide first aid and do self-rescue to feel safe and at ease.

Living off the grid calls for a greater capacity for independence and flexibility. An attitude of preparedness, resilience, and attentiveness toward the challenges and rewards of living in distant and untamed places is developed as personal safety and security become fundamental parts of the way of life.

Non-Firearm Self-Defense Techniques

Self-defense methods that don't involve firearms cover many mental and physical ploys to keep you safe. These methods, which draw on the tenets of several martial arts, prioritize situational awareness, clear and concise communication, and using one's body to diffuse potentially dangerous situations and keep people safe.

Non-lethal self-defense relies heavily on martial arts training. For self-defense, practitioners hone their striking, blocking, and grappling skills. Martial arts training improves physical fitness and mental fortitude in the face of adversity.

Self-defense relies heavily on being aware of one's surroundings. Awareness of one's environment helps people spot danger, avoid it, and take preventative measures to keep themselves safe. When people are more alert, they are better able to take appropriate action when threatened.

One effective method of non-lethal self-defense is verbal de-escalation. Learning to speak up and assert yourself quietly can prevent fights from escalating. Learning to express oneself clearly, stand up for one's rights, and find peaceful solutions to conflicts require strong communication skills.

Self-defense experts agree that evasion and escape skills are crucial. Individuals can learn to avoid danger and seek safety by knowing how to establish distance from a potential threat, using cover effectively, and locating escape routes.

Confidence in oneself and physical appearance can go a long way toward warding off would-be assailants. Making oneself appear less vulnerable and less likely to be targeted can be accomplished by using body language, including making and keeping eye contact and strolling confidently.

It is important to focus on weak points when using non-lethal means of protection. If you're in a physical altercation with someone, it's best to aim for their weak spots, such as their eyes, nose, neck, or crotch.

Self-defense techniques that make use of commonplace items are also a viable option. It's a good idea for everyone to know how to use everyday objects like keys, umbrellas, and bags as improvised weapons.

Learning effective means of self-defense through formal instruction is essential. Self-defense seminars and workshops focusing on non-lethal techniques can help people learn how to defend themselves and their loved ones.

Avoiding dangerous situations is a cornerstone of weapon-free self-defense. People try to avoid harm by taking the most direct route, being extra cautious in strange places, and going with their gut feelings.

Self-defense relies heavily on mental preparedness. One's ability to keep cool under pressure and make quick decisions in trying situations is greatly enhanced by cultivating a mindset of self-reliance, readiness, and the determination to act when necessary.

Self-defense methods that do not involve firearms emphasize keeping oneself and others safe without violence. Confidence in the face of danger can be achieved through the development of situational awareness, the ability to communicate effectively, and the possession of physical abilities.

Securing the Off-Grid Shelter and Resources

One of the most important parts of off-the-grid sustainability is ensuring your home and supplies are safe and sound. People living off the grid must be self-sufficient and take precautions to protect their homes, possessions, and resources.

Securing the actual dwelling is a major issue for people living independently of the power grid. Off-the-grid homes are typically situated in remote places, where intruders or wild animals are more likely to attack them. As a result, those living away from the grid have taken various precautions to ensure their safety. Common methods of deterring would-be intruders include shoring up weak points (such as doors and windows), setting up artificial (such as motion-detecting lights and security cameras), and natural (such as fences and thorny bushes) barriers.

To successfully live off the grid, you must have reliable access to clean water. People who live off the grid typically collect water by digging wells or using natural springs. Maintaining a steady water supply requires constant attention to detail, including installing effective filtration systems and maintaining all available water sources.

Proper food storage and preservation methods are necessary to prevent waste and deterioration. Root cellars, coolers, and food dehydrators are common tools for those living off the grid to preserve food. Protect against rodents by using rodent-proof containers and keeping food off the ground.

It is equally important to safeguard off-grid supplies against natural disasters. Off-grid settlements are vulnerable to fires, floods, and extreme weather events. Essential measures for protecting resources include creating firebreaks, making buildings more weatherproof, and developing contingency plans.

Off-grid communities rely on renewable energy sources like solar panels, wind turbines, and generators to power their homes. Keeping energy infrastructure safe means preventing losses due to vandalism or theft. Energy efficiency measures and backup systems can prevent disruptions caused by a loss of power.

Off-grid communities' safety depends on people being in touch with one another. It's common for neighbors to help and support one another. Together, we can better deal with possible dangers by setting up neighborhood watch programs and emergency communication lines.

Protecting agricultural resources is essential for developing a self-sufficient way of life. Using organic pest control and perimeter fences to protect wildlife from crops is possible in off-grid settlements.

Primarily, alertness and preparedness are required when securing off-grid housing and resources. Those living off the grid must constantly evaluate threats, adjust to new information, and monitor local conditions. Off-grid communities can construct a secure and long-lasting home in harmony with nature by using commonsense security measures and keeping a strong and supportive community.

1. **If you haven't already done so, scan the QR code at the beginning of the book** and download THE BEST SURVIVAL DIY PROJECTS eBook + VIDEOS.

2. **Scan the QR code below and leave quick feedback on Amazon!**

SCAN ME

Book 9:

Essential Skills for Survival in the Wild

Those who make it through life's hardships in the wild have mastered a wide range of abilities that have proven crucial to their success. Knowledge of nature, independence, and flexibility are all part of these abilities, which are necessary for survival in every environment.

Knowing where and how to get safe drinking water is a necessity, first and foremost. Safe drinking water can be obtained by locating and tapping natural water sources like streams or springs and then purifying that water through methods like boiling or filtration.

Building a fire is the second most important skill for surviving in the wilderness. The capacity to make fire is essential for survival because it provides heat, deters predators, allows for the preparation of food, and gives people a feeling of safety. Lighting a fire using numerous means, such as friction, flint, steel, or a magnifying glass, is critical.

Knowing how to construct a safe haven in the wilderness is also important. A safe location to relax and protect from the elements can be ensured by building a shelter from natural materials such as branches, leaves, or animal hides.

To survive in the wild, you must learn to forage for food and recognize edible plants. It's important to identify which plants are safe to consume to avoid poisoning and provide a steady supply of nutritious food.

The ability to hunt and trap is a necessity for obtaining sufficient protein. Successful hunting is more likely if one is proficient with traps, tracking, and archery equipment.

The ability to navigate one's way about in the outdoors is essential. It is possible to keep one's bearings and prevent loss by using natural landmarks, the sun, the stars, and a compass.

Knowing how to administer basic first aid in the event of an injury or medical emergency while out in the wilderness is crucial. In a survival situation, the ability to treat wounds, burns, and other common ailments might be crucial.

Long-term existence necessitates the ability to adjust to yearly climate shifts. Protecting one's health requires understanding how to plan for weather events like storms and heat waves.

Positivity and mental toughness are just as crucial for making it alive in the wild. Overcoming obstacles and keeping optimism alive requires a strong will, creativity, and composure in adversity.

Last but not least, sustainable survival requires an appreciation of nature and its inhabitants. This ideal includes protecting wildlife, maintaining natural resources, and otherwise coexisting with the natural world.

Meeting one's basic needs and navigating the obstacles presented by nature necessitates a wide range of critical abilities for surviving in the wild. Individuals can flourish and develop a meaningful relationship with the outdoors by preparing themselves with information, being flexible, and keeping a happy attitude.

Getting your Bearings Without Modern Technology

The capacity to "get your bearings" without using modern technology, such as a GPS or a smartphone, refers to finding one's way around uncharted areas or the woods. Using only one's senses and the environment around them, one can learn to orient themselves and return to a previously visited spot.

It's important to use the sun as a natural compass. The cardinal directions can be found by watching the sun rise and set. The sun rises in the eastern sky and sets on the western horizon in the Northern Hemisphere. The opposite is true in the Southern Hemisphere. When the sun is directly overhead in the middle of the day, it tends to line up with the equator.

Similarly, at night, the stars can be used as a guide. The North Star (Polaris) is a solid indicator of direction because it is close to the North Pole and seems relatively fixed in the sky. Using other star patterns and constellations to find the four cardinal directions is possible.

The use of geographical features as navigational aids is another viable option. Understanding your location on a map is as simple as looking around at the arrangement of mountains, rivers, coastlines, and other prominent terrain elements.

The direction of the wind is another simple sign of direction. It is possible to infer cardinal directions based on the direction of the wind in many regions over long periods.

Animal behavior can serve as a useful navigational aid. Animals like bees and birds have an innate sense of direction that they can use to help others find food and water. Studying animal tracks is another way to gain insight into possible routes.

Making and using cairns or other easily identifiable trail markers will help you find your way back along the route you've already taken.

Finally, reading a topographic map and familiarity with the area is crucial for navigating without technology. You can compare what you see in the world to what the map depicts with the help of a topographic map, which details things like elevation, terrain characteristics, and landmarks.

Navigating without the aid of technology calls for a honed capacity for observation, familiarity with natural elements and navigational indications, and reliance on fundamental resources like the sun, stars, natural landmarks, and topographic maps. As a result of practicing these abilities, people may easily travel through uncharted territory and experience a more meaningful connection to the natural environment.

Lighting Fires Without Matches or Lighters

The ability to ignite a fire using only natural resources and time-honored techniques is a crucial survival skill. Knowing how to build a fire without access to contemporary fire-starting tools is vital in times of crisis, outdoor expeditions, and off-the-grid settings. Learning how to make fire from scratch using only the materials you find in nature is possible thanks to the evolution of several ancient fire-making techniques.

The bow drill is the most well-known device for creating friction fire. A wooden spindle is rotated against a fireboard using a wooden bow. The heat of friction can ignite a fire by moving an ember to a tinder bundle.

The earliest known method of making fire involved a piece of steel or iron and flint or other hard rock used as a striker. A bundle of fuel or burned material can be set ablaze by these sparks.

It is possible to start a fire by rubbing a wooden plow against a dry wooden base or fireboard, which generates enough friction and heat to produce an ember.

To start a fire using a fire saw, you would use a sawing motion on a dry piece of wood, much like a fire plow.

Fire by Lens: Concentrating sunlight to create heat and fire a tinder bundle with a magnifying glass, a clear plastic bag filled with water, or a spherical chunk of ice.

Compressed air is used to ignite charred material, which can then be transported to a tinder bundle using a device called a fire piston.

Each approach calls for diligent training and high-quality Tinder and kindling selection. Making a fire requires correct preparation of the fire lay, which involves arranging tinder, kindling, and fuel.

Remember that starting a fire the old-fashioned way can be difficult, especially in bad weather or when you need more supplies. If you know how to start a fire and have some dry tinder and kindling, you can do so without resorting to matches or lighters.

The ability to start a fire without any artificial means strengthens a person's independence and ability to adapt to their natural environment. As a connecting link between the past and the present, fire-building traditions help people develop a better appreciation for their ancestors' gifts.

1. **If you haven't already done so, scan the QR code at the beginning of the book** and download THE BEST SURVIVAL DIY PROJECTS eBook + VIDEOS.

2. **Scan the QR code below and leave quick feedback on Amazon!**

SCAN ME

Book 10:

Urban Survival Strategies

"urban survival strategies" refers to various practices that help people stay safe and secure in high-density urban environments. City life's challenges and opportunities differ from those of the wilderness, and urban survival training reflects this.

Being ready for an emergency is crucial for life in the city. An emergency kit with food, water, first aid supplies, and a flashlight is important to be prepared for any situation. It is also important to be aware of potential dangers, have a strategy for communicating with loved ones, and be familiar with evacuation routes.

Knowing how to get around in a city is crucial. To avoid getting stuck in traffic or lost in an emergency, it helps to know the city's structure, familiarize yourself with alternate routes, and memorize important landmarks.

For urban existence, careful resource management is essential. Learning to ration and make the most of scarce resources is essential for long-term survival in highly populated locations.

Self-defense and awareness of your surroundings are crucial to your city's safety. Knowing how to defend oneself and keep one's wits about one in a city where one may face criminals or confrontations.

In the event of a disaster, it is important to know how to stay in place in case it is not safe or practicable to evacuate. Securing a space, protecting doors and windows, and conserving supplies are vital for long periods spent indoors.

During urban catastrophes, clean water may take a lot of work. Maintaining adequate hydration and health necessitates proficiently purifying water from various sources, including rainwater and natural bodies of water.

During times of crisis, it might not be easy to find food in urban areas. Finding additional food sources is easier if people know where to go for community gardens, urban farms, and edible wild plants.

To thrive in a city, you need to be able to talk to people and make connections. Building relationships with neighbors and community members facilitates sharing resources, knowledge, and assistance during emergencies.

The ability to change and shift plans quickly is key in urban survival situations. Successfully navigating unanticipated hurdles requires adapting to shifting circumstances and generating novel approaches to old problems.

Keeping a low profile might be helpful in dangerous or dangerously unpredictable situations. Keeping one's cool, avoiding unwanted attention, and prioritizing one's safety are all important factors in making life in the city unscathed.

Planning for urban survival is important at any time, not just in the aftermath of a major catastrophe. Acquiring the requisite information and skills can improve self-reliance, readiness, and confidence to deal with unexpected situations in urban settings.

Navigating Emergencies in Urban Environments

One must have a certain set of skills and methods to effectively respond to the wide range of crisis scenarios that may arise in highly crowded urban areas. Natural disasters, civil unrest, terrorist assaults, and accidents fall into this category. The best way to secure one's and others' safety in dangerous situations is to come prepared with a solid game plan.

First, it's essential to have a plan in place for dealing with unexpected situations. Preparing for a disaster means stocking up on food, water, first aid supplies, lighting, and communication tools. Ensuring everyone is safe during emergencies requires knowing evacuation routes and a predetermined meeting place.

Being aware of your surroundings is crucial in busy cities. The ability to recognize threats and dangers in one's environment depends on one's level of vigilance and awareness. You can keep yourself safe by watching for strange behavior and staying away from potentially dangerous regions.

It can be challenging to make your way across crowded city streets in an emergency. When regular roads are closed or otherwise impassable, people who know the city's layout, know how to discover alternative routes and have maps or GPS devices on hand are more likely to reach their destinations safely.

It may be safer to stay put and wait out an emergency than to try to flee. When staying indoors for an extended period, it is important to secure the area, reinforce the doors and windows, and limit the use of utilities.

When dealing with a crisis in a city, good communication is more important than ever. People can keep up with the situation and get updates from authorities if they have access to several forms of communication, such as cell phones, radios, and emergency alert systems.

It is crucial to avoid hotspots of conflict and violence during civil unrest or terrorist strikes. Individuals can protect themselves by avoiding protest locations or other active danger zones and taking refuge in safe buildings.

It can be difficult to locate potable water in an urban emergency. Knowing how to purify water from different sources like rainfall or existing water fixtures is essential in times of crisis.

In an emergency, finding food in a city may require some ingenuity. Individuals and families can be sustained by locating food resources such as neighborhood food banks or shelters and knowing where to get non-perishable foods in stores.

Being ready to shift your plans on the fly is essential in emergencies in the city. Keeping oneself safe in the face of unforeseen circumstances often necessitates improvising and making snap decisions.

Lastly, building resilience in the face of urban calamities requires cooperation between neighbors and community members. It is easier to respond to emergencies when people work together, help one another, and join community watch groups.

It takes a blend of forethought, situational awareness, flexibility, and clear speech to get through an emergency in a city. Successfully overcoming obstacles and guaranteeing personal safety in densely populated regions requires having a well-thought-out plan and the capacity to make intelligent judgments in high-stress situations.

Adapting Off-Grid Techniques to City Life

If you want to live more independently and sustainably in an urban area, you'll need to adopt off-grid tactics, which are more typical of rural areas. Despite the obvious differences between city life and off-grid existence, there are ways in which off-grid concepts and abilities can help make cities safer, greener, and more resilient.

Energy conservation is one of the most fundamental off-grid practices that can be transferred to city living. Power expenses and carbon emissions can be reduced in urban areas by switching to energy-efficient appliances, using natural light better, and tweaking heating and cooling setups.

Another off-the-grid method useful in urban settings is collecting rainwater for later use. Collecting rainwater from roofs and its subsequent use in non-potable applications, such as watering plants and flushing toilets, helps reduce the strain on municipal water systems.

Among the many off-grid practices that find a home in urban areas is gardening. Connecting with nature and getting your hands dirty go hand in hand when cultivating your veggies and herbs on your balcony, roof, or community garden.

Composting is an off-the-grid technique that can be adapted to city life to lessen the amount of garbage sent to landfills and provide nutrient-rich soil for city gardens. Creating a more environmentally friendly waste management system is one of the many benefits of composting food scraps and yard trash.

Sustainable living can be encouraged, and energy efficiency can be increased by constructing or remodeling homes using eco-friendly materials and designs. More sustainable urban housing can be achieved by using recycled or repurposed materials and adopting passive solar design concepts.

Reducing the need for bottled water and enhancing city water quality are possible outcomes of implementing off-grid water purifying methods. Access to safe drinking water can be ensured by installing water filtration equipment or using portable water purifiers.

Basic first aid and self-defense are two off-the-grid skills useful anywhere and can make city living feel safer. Self-defense training and medical literacy education give people the tools to act responsibly in times of crisis.

Incorporating some off-grid habits can help make city life more sustainable, resilient, and ecologically conscientious. At the same time, city life may need to afford a different level of self-sufficiency than off-grid living. Individuals can contribute to the environment and their communities while embracing the values of self-reliance and sustainability by combining these tactics with modern urban amenities and infrastructure.

1. **If you haven't already done so, scan the QR code at the beginning of the book** and download THE BEST SURVIVAL DIY PROJECTS eBook + VIDEOS.

2. **Scan the QR code below and leave quick feedback on Amazon!**

SCAN ME

Book 11:

Winter Survival Techniques

A person's ability to survive and even thrive in extreme cold directly correlates to their knowledge of winter survival practices. Extreme cold, fewer hours of sunshine, and the possibility of severe weather like snow or ice storms are just a few of the difficulties that winter brings. Winter outdoor activities can be fun and rewarding, but only if you know how to remain warm, get food and water, and keep yourself safe.

Preventing hypothermia and keeping warm throughout the cold is essential. Protect yourself against the cold by dressing in several layers, donning an insulated and waterproof outer layer, and accessorizing with hats, gloves, and scarves. Shelters or well-insulated tents are necessary for a good night's sleep and protection from the weather.

Knowing how to start a fire in the snow or rain is essential for winter survival. Fire is essential because it may be used for heating, lighting, and cooking. Successful fire-making requires familiarity with various fire-starting procedures, including using dry fuel, fire starters, and constructing a fire reflector.

In the winter, finding a reliable water source might be difficult because many natural water sources are either frozen or unavailable. It is crucial to understand how to safely melt snow and ice for drinking water and then purify it using filters or boiling.

Finding food in the winter demands ingenuity. Knowing how to ice fish, build traps, or forage for edible wild plants are all useful skills in times of food need. A winter survival kit should also include high-energy snacks and nonperishable consumables.

Whiteout circumstances make it exceptionally difficult to see your way through snow-covered landscapes. The ability to keep your bearings and find your way back depends on your familiarity with using landmarks, compasses, and global positioning systems.

Being ready for unexpected events is essential for survival in the cold. In an emergency, having access to first aid supplies, signaling devices, a map, and a means of communication can mean the difference between life and death in the winter.

It is crucial for safety reasons to know about winter hazards like avalanches and frostbite and how to prevent or treat them. Individuals can better prepare for and respond to hazardous conditions if they are familiar with winter weather forecasts and pay attention to weather changes.

Having strong mental makeup is essential for making it through the winter. Having a can-do attitude, being flexible, and keeping your cool under pressure are all qualities that will help you make it through trying situations.

Preparedness, resourcefulness, and knowledge are the three pillars of winter survival. Even in the worst winter circumstances, people can tackle problems head-on and enjoy outdoor activities if they take the necessary precautions to keep warm, have access to food and water, know how to navigate and solve emergencies and keep their minds in the game.

Heating and Insulation in Challenging Climates

To create cozy, energy-efficient homes in harsh climates, heating, and insulation are crucial for building design and upkeep. Extreme seasonal temperature swings make it difficult to keep a comfortable indoor temperature in climates with very frigid winters or hot summers.

Keeping homes warm and cozy in harsh winters is all about reliability and efficiency. Central heating, wood-burning stoves, electric heaters, and radiant floor heating are only some methods for maintaining a suitable indoor climate. It is crucial to pick a heating system that can cope with the low temperatures in really cold regions.

Insulation is essential for keeping warm and decreasing energy loss in colder areas. Insulated walls, ceilings, and floors keep warm air inside during the winter and cool air inside during the summer. Insulation is typically installed with common materials like fiberglass, cellulose, foam board, or spray foam. Double-paned or thermal windows also help with this problem.

Pipe insulation is a necessity in extremely cold areas. Frozen and burst pipes are less likely to occur when plumbing is properly insulated in unheated places such as basements and crawl spaces.

Insulation and heat control are both crucial in extremely hot climes. Reduce the need for air conditioning by using highly insulating walls and windows, reflective roofing materials, shading devices like awnings or sunscreens, and natural ventilation.

Passive solar design can use the sun's warmth during the winter and protect against its intensity during the summer in regions where temperatures fluctuate widely. This method of architecture takes advantage of the prevailing weather patterns to achieve maximum efficiency and comfort.

Heating, ventilation, and air conditioning (HVAC) systems are especially important in regions that experience extremes of temperature throughout the year. These systems must heat the space sufficiently during cold spells and cool it effectively during hot spells.

Maintaining a comfortable indoor climate while decreasing energy use and utility costs is possible with the help of energy-efficient HVAC systems, insulation, and weatherization.

Choosing heating systems that can withstand extreme temperatures, utilizing efficient insulation materials, and adopting passive solar design concepts when applicable are the cornerstones of successful heating and insulation in harsh regions. Comfortable and energy-efficient housing is possible even in locations with wide temperature swings, provided precautions are taken to insulate buildings, prevent pipes from freezing, and control solar heat gain. By combining these strategies, people will be better able to endure harsh climates while reducing their negative effects on the ecosystem and energy needs.

Storing Food and Resources for Harsh Winters

A crucial part of being self-reliant and sustainable for individuals or communities living in distant and isolated areas is storing food and supplies for hard winters in an off-the-grid context. Since people living off the grid must rely on their resources to meet their daily needs, they must take extra precautions during the winter months, when things like electricity, water, and food may be in short supply.

Preserving food through canning and preserving is a frequent off-grid method used to save food for the winter. Many people who live off the grid cultivate their food during the warmer months and can pickle, ferment, or dehydrate the harvest to enjoy throughout the year. A consistent supply of healthy food over the winter can be ensured by storing these preserved items in a cold, dry place.

Off-the-grid situations make the most use of root cellars. Root vegetables, winter squashes, and other crops that can sustain off-grid folks throughout the winter can be stored in these underground storage areas because of the low and consistent temperature they maintain. A dependable and efficient storage environment can be created with proper insulation and ventilation in a root cellar.

Some people living off the grid, especially those with access to consistent solar or alternate energy sources, can freeze food. These situations call for solar-powered freezers to keep food from spoiling throughout the winter.

Living off the grid, where access to commercial supermarkets may be limited, necessitates dry food storage. A reliable food supply through the winter and beyond can be ensured by stocking up on dry goods such as grains, beans, rice, and pasta. Keeping them in Mylar bags or other airtight containers keeps them dry and pest-free.

Off-grid living requires more than just food storage. Firewood is essential for winter heating and cooking, so stocking up before the cold sets in is important. A good supply of firewood is essential for those living off the grid, as they must use wood to heat their homes during the cold months.

People who live off the grid must stockpile not only food and firewood but also things like generator fuel, batteries, candles, and medical supplies. Being completely self-sufficient is essential for off-the-grid life. Therefore, stocking up on these items before you need them is important.

Communities that live off the grid typically store their resources in a central location. Neighbors can help one another by pooling resources and working together to face the harsh winter. Community initiatives to store food and pool scarce supplies help off-the-grid settlements weather the winter.

In off-grid settings, keeping an organized stockpile of supplies is essential. The quality and freshness of resources in storage can be maintained through routine inspections and the rotation of supply, which ensures that older products are used first.

In conclusion, preparing for hard winters off the grid needs planning, preservation techniques, and group effort to store food and resources. Success in inaccessible regions, especially during the harsh winter, requires a commitment to self-sufficiency, sustainability, and community cooperation.

1. **If you haven't already done so, scan the QR code at the beginning of the book** and download THE BEST SURVIVAL DIY PROJECTS eBook + VIDEOS.

2. **Scan the QR code below and leave quick feedback on Amazon!**

SCAN ME

Book 12:

The Ethics of Off-Grid Survival

Individuals and communities pursuing self-sufficiency and sustainable living in distant and isolated areas are guided by a set of core ideas and values known as the ethics of off-grid survival. Important environmental, social responsibility and value-based questions arise from the reduced reliance on conventional utility networks and external resources that characterize this way of living.

Environmental care is important to off-the-grid survival ethics. Sustainable practices, such as using renewable energy, reducing water use, and using environmentally friendly farming methods, are utilized by those striving to lessen their negative environmental effects. The ethical off-grid lifestyle places a premium on preserving the natural world for future generations.

The value of independence and agency is also central to off-the-grid survival ethics. To achieve self-sufficiency, an individual or group must acquire the knowledge and abilities to meet their basic requirements without external help. Self-sufficiency is morally commendable since it promotes self-improvement, autonomy, and less reliance on institutionalized authority.

Off-the-gridders must treat the environment with reverence. Respecting and protecting the natural world is a moral imperative. To that end, professionals take precautions not to kill animals, upset ecosystems, or hasten the deterioration of the natural world.

While off-the-grid living promotes independence, it also requires consideration for others. This includes things like respecting surrounding communities, following the rules, and making a beneficial impact on society when engaging in off-the-grid activities.

Some people who live off the grid base their moral compass on community and working together. Promoting open and honest group decision-making, cooperation, and mutual aid are all ethically important.

Ethical issues also arise when balancing off-the-grid lifestyle and other features of contemporary life. While staying true to the tenets of off-the-grid life, ethical practitioners acknowledge the benefits of technological advancement and societal understanding.

Off-the-grid survivalists hold to the ethical ideals of preparedness and readiness to aid others. Practitioners plan for and respond to emergencies and help their communities and neighbors by pooling their resources and knowledge in times of need.

The ethics of off-grid survival boil down to acting by one's values and principles. Those living off the grid do so after carefully considering how their lifestyle choices align with their most cherished values.

The ethics of off-grid survival are multifaceted and include considerations of the environment, independence, community, and one's moral compass. By adhering to these ethical standards, people and groups can adopt an off-the-grid way of living that is both sustainable and meaningful, taking into account greater social concerns while respecting nature, community, and personal autonomy.

Responsible Environmental and Social Practices

As more and more people strive for sustainable, off-the-grid lifestyles, engaging in environmentally and socially responsible behaviors is more important than ever. In an off-the-grid setting, these habits are significant for various reasons, including damage prevention, resource conservation, community building, and maintaining peace and happiness.

Reducing one's ecological footprint by adopting sustainable living habits is important to environmentally responsible off-grid survival. Off-grid systems can reduce their dependency on fossil fuels by adopting renewable energy sources like solar panels and wind turbines. Reducing resource consumption and waste generation also requires implementing energy-efficient equipment and using effective waste management, recycling, and composting procedures.

Off-the-grid survivalists place a high value on protecting the environment. For example, you could use methods that cause less harm to the local flora and animals and respect wildlife habitats. Land that has been properly cared for will continue to provide for future generations.

Water conservation is especially important when living off the grid because of the potential for scarcity. Water conservation measures can be implemented in the home, and help reduce the amount of water used for cooking, cleaning, and showering.

In the context of off-grid survival, social responsibility is just as crucial. A strong and welcoming off-grid community results from its members treating one another with dignity and working together to solve problems.

Fairness and equality in resource distribution and decision-making are essential tenets of off-the-grid social activities that promote social responsibility. By encouraging people to share their ideas and participate in community decision-making, we strengthen our group's bonds of trust and cooperation.

Interactions with nearby communities or indigenous peoples also fall within the purview of socially responsible behavior. Those who live off the grid should work with their neighbors, respect their rights, and be a productive part of the community.

Personal development is facilitated, and social relationships are strengthened when the off-grid community supports learning and skills exchange. Providing people opportunities to learn new things strengthens their independence and capacity to bounce back from setbacks.

When living off the grid, contributing to the local community's well-being and supporting local initiatives are cornerstones of social interaction. Volunteering, participating in community initiatives, and helping out in times of crisis all foster a strong sense of community and mutual aid.

Sustainability, resource conservation, social fairness, and community development are important to off-the-grid survival and environmentally and socially responsible activities. In addition to building a social environment that values inclusion and collaboration, these behaviors allow off-grid individuals or communities to flourish harmoniously with nature. Off-the-grid survivalists can have a long-lasting, beneficial effect on the world around them if they act with awareness and consideration.

Living Harmoniously with Nature

In the context of off-grid survival, "living harmoniously with nature" refers to behaviors that prioritize the conservation of resources, acceptance of a sustainable lifestyle, and the prevention of environmental damage. To ensure their survival, off-the-grid survivalists work to foster a mutually beneficial relationship with the natural world.

Off-grid survival requires using sustainable energy sources to minimize negative environmental impacts. We can lessen our impact on the environment and the economy by using renewable energy sources like solar panels, wind turbines, and hydroelectric dams. Those living off the grid can lessen their environmental impact by switching to renewable energy sources like solar and wind.

Living in peace with nature also requires practicing responsible land management. Off-the-grid survivalists emphasized organic farming and permaculture practices that are environmentally friendly. Improving soil health and providing a sustainable food supply means implementing crop rotation, soil regeneration, and biodiversity conservation practices.

In an off-the-grid setting, water conservation is critical. If you want to reduce your environmental impact and live in harmony with the natural world, treat water as a scarce resource and implement conservation measures like collecting rainwater and reusing used water.

Off-the-grid survivalists prioritize reducing trash and increasing their use of composting and recycling. Natural resources may be protected, and people can do their part by reusing things and decreasing landfill trash.

One method to do this is to construct off-the-grid homes that blend in with the scenery. Buildings that use passive solar design principles and locally sourced, organic materials have a smaller environmental and social footprint.

In off-grid survival, learning to live harmoniously with nature means using resources wisely. To conserve the few resources, those who live off the grid put their necessities ahead of their wants.

To lessen the negative effects of humans on the natural world, it is crucial to observe responsible outdoor ethics like the leave-no-trace principle and to protect wildlife habitats. To protect ecological systems, off-the-grid survivalists try to live peacefully with wildlife.

Developing a respect for nature is integral to eco-friendly living. People who live off the grid frequently gain a strong regard for the interconnectivity of all living things because of their closeness to the earth and its cycles.

Sustainable practices, renewable energy, ethical land management, and conscious resource consumption are fundamental to off-the-grid survival and achieving harmony with nature. Off-the-grid survivalists can help improve the world by adopting a lifestyle that works in harmony with nature. This will protect the planet's fragile ecosystems and make it stronger.

1. **If you haven't already done so, scan the QR code at the beginning of the book** and download THE BEST SURVIVAL DIY PROJECTS eBook + VIDEOS.

2. **Scan the QR code below and leave quick feedback on Amazon!**

SCAN ME

Book 13:

Waste Management and Recycling

Sustainable activities that attempt to lessen their negative effects on the environment, save scarce resources, and send as little trash as possible to landfills and incinerators inherently include waste management and recycling programs. Environmentally responsible and resource-conserving waste management strategies include collection, disposal, and processing.

Waste management is the process of overseeing all aspects of garbage, from collection to storage to disposal. Creating manageable waste streams for disposal and recycling requires sorting trash into organic, recyclable, and non-recyclable categories.

One of the most important aspects of waste management is recycling, which is making new products out of old ones to lessen the need for primary resources and power. Paper, glass, plastic, metal, and some electronics can all be recycled. Recycling lessens the negative effects of trash disposal on the environment by conserving natural resources and cutting down on emissions of greenhouse gases.

Different regions and garbage types necessitate distinct approaches to waste collection and disposal. Household and commercial trash is often collected and taken to local landfills or recycling plants. These centers sort trash by type and recyclability, then dispose of it by composting, incineration, or landfill.

Facilities dedicated to recycling collect recyclables and process them so they can be used again in production. Paper may be reused to make other paper goods, plastic can be repurposed to make other plastic products, and metal can be recycled and used in various manufacturing processes.

Public education and involvement are essential to successful waste management and recycling initiatives. The best way to promote responsible behavior is to inform people about the significance of recycling, waste reduction, and safe waste disposal.

Some areas encourage recycling by instituting deposit-return schemes or other forms of financial compensation for residents who bring in bottles and cans for recycling.

Contamination is a major problem in recycling and waste management. When recyclables are contaminated with non-recyclable elements, sorting and reusing them becomes more hassle. The spread of accurate information and the establishment of uniform standards for recycling can assist in reducing this issue.

When taken as a whole, waste management and recycling greatly help the environment and conserve resources. Communities and people may help create a cleaner, healthier environment and a more sustainable future by reducing waste, reusing products, and recycling as much as possible.

Eco-Friendly Waste Disposal Practices

We're referring to eco-friendly waste disposal procedures when discussing sustainable trash management and reducing our environmental footprint. Reduced trash generation, increased recycling, and environmentally sound waste treatment are at the heart of these sustainable practices.

Source reduction is an important part of an environmentally responsible waste management strategy. Waste can be reduced if people and businesses make more eco-friendly purchasing decisions and use less disposable or overly-packaged goods. This method lessens the load on landfills and other waste-handling facilities.

Recycling is the cornerstone of eco-friendly garbage disposal. By recovering recyclables from the trash stream, we can process and reuse them, cutting down on the manufacturing process's need for new raw materials and energy. Contributing to a circular economy and reducing the demand for new resource extraction, recycling paper, plastics, glass, and metals.

One more environmentally friendly way to handle organic waste is by composting. Food scraps, yard clippings, and other biodegradable items can be composted to produce nutrient-rich compost, which can then be utilized to improve agricultural land.

Using waste-to-energy techniques to recover energy from non-recyclable garbage is an environmentally friendly option. Reducing dependency on fossil fuels and greenhouse gas emissions, these technologies turn garbage into useful energy.

Anaerobic digestion, which creates biogas from organic waste, and adopting smart trash sorting technologies are two innovative waste management methods that contribute to more environmentally friendly garbage disposal.

Promoting environmentally responsible waste management strategies requires widespread participation and education. Sustainable waste management practices are adopted by individuals and businesses when educational programs and efforts highlight trash reduction, recycling, and appropriate disposal.

For change to occur on a societal level, legislation and policies that encourage using environmentally friendly trash disposal methods are crucial. Governments and organizations can encourage recycling by providing financial incentives, setting waste reduction goals, and regulating waste treatment procedures.

Proper trash segregation and waste collecting systems are also essential to effective eco-friendly waste disposal methods. Materials can be more easily treated and recycled if separated into their respective categories using designated bins for recyclables, organic garbage, and other trash.

A more sustainable and cleaner environment results from people and organizations adopting eco-friendly trash disposal procedures. By easing the burden on the planet's natural resources, protecting its ecosystems, and lessening the damage that waste causes, these methods help ensure a brighter and more sustainable future for everyone.

Creative Recycling Solutions for Off-Grid Living

Off-grid communities rely heavily on resource conservation and long-term sustainability, making it imperative that residents find innovative ways to recycle their waste. People living off the grid often resort to novel recycling methods and reusing old items to make the most of their scarce resources.

Off-grinders frequently recycle and use existing materials to extend the useful life of products and lessen the demand for new resources. Recycling and resourcefulness can be seen in using old wooden pallets for new furniture or making compost bins from old barrels.

Repurposing an old shipping container into a new home or storage unit is a sustainable and resourceful way to meet those requirements. Building with recycled materials conserves resources, as there is less need to buy new materials (which might be expensive or scarce in off-grid areas).

The scope of resourceful recycling goes much beyond that of buildings. Glass jars and containers can be reused for food storage by those living off the grid, eliminating their need for disposable plastic containers. Repurposing discarded clothes and fabric remnants by making quilts and other textile projects is another example of creative recycling.

Off-grid communities often come up with novel energy solutions through inventive recycling. For example: using used automobile batteries to store energy in solar-powered devices increases their useful life and lessens their negative impact on the environment.

In addition, many tools and decorations used by those who live off the grid are made from scrap metal. Artistic ingenuity and clever recycling can be displayed when discarded tools or industrial pieces are transformed into one-of-a-kind sculptures or put to new, useful ends.

Ingenious recycling methods for off-the-grid dwellings sometimes include composting. Creating compost from organic waste improves soil quality and promotes sustainable farming practices. Composting eliminates the need for synthetic fertilizers in off-grid gardens.

Rainwater can be collected and stored in barrels or tanks, another example of resourceful recycling in the off-grid setting. Off-grid residents can save money and lessen their environmental impact by collecting and using rainwater.

Off-grid communities can encourage an innovative and resourceful mindset by participating in skill-sharing and recycling projects. Collective efforts towards sustainability are strengthened when members are encouraged to share their innovative recycling ideas and skills.

Off-grid communities place a premium on minimizing waste and maximizing sustainability. Therefore, inventive recycling methods are crucial. Individuals living off the grid show resourcefulness and contribute to a more sustainable and harmonious way of life in harmony with nature by repurposing materials, building inventive structures, reusing ordinary objects, and turning trash into precious resources.

1. **If you haven't already done so, scan the QR code at the beginning of the book** and download THE BEST SURVIVAL DIY PROJECTS eBook + VIDEOS.

2. **Scan the QR code below and leave quick feedback on Amazon!**

SCAN ME

Book 14:

Building a Thriving Off-Grid Community

A community's commitment to sustainability and self-sufficiency, together with a common vision and the willingness to work together, are essential to the success of any off-grid endeavor. A strong sense of community and mutual support is fostered when people work together to build a safe and secure place to call home.

A healthy off-grid community is built on shared goals and values. People gather here because they want to practice sustainable lifestyles that also respect the environment and are independent of outside resources. This common goal underpins effective decision-making, productive collaboration, and sustainable community development.

Building trust and solidarity among residents requires open communication lines and fair decision-making procedures. To establish a sense of ownership and enable individuals to contribute to the development of the community, it is important to encourage open communication and involve all members in decision-making.

Off-grid communities prioritizing sustainability in their infrastructure and land use tend to thrive. The community can reduce its environmental impact by planning and creating buildings using renewable energy systems and environmentally safe materials. Sustainable farming is made possible through responsible land management, such as permaculture techniques, which also value and protect the local ecology.

Developing a strong community in an off-the-grid location relies heavily on exchanging information and expertise. Residents provide various abilities, including sustainable farming and building, renewable energy, and expert artisanal craftsmanship. Workshops and other educational events that promote the exchange of knowledge and skills help individuals gain independence while bolstering the community.

An off-the-grid society can only succeed through cooperation and mutual aid. Locals commonly believe that working together builds resilience and prosperity for all. Cooperation and friendship flourish when people help one another in need, work together on initiatives, and share their resources.

Social events and festivities foster a strong sense of community and belonging. Sharing in common experiences like feasts, celebrations, or artistic endeavors strengthens bonds between neighbors and improves the quality of life for everyone.

A healthy off-grid community also benefits from establishing relationships with nearby villages. One can expand their network of friends, acquaintances, and potential helpers by participating in regional activities, working on projects, and attending local events.

A successful off-the-grid society can only be built on mutual respect and acceptance of one another's differences. Communities that welcome and value people from all walks of life and points of view are stronger and more cohesive.

Finally, an off-grid community will thrive in the long run if its members are willing to be flexible and adapt. The capacity to adapt and discover creative solutions together means the community may thrive even in difficult conditions, such as when weather patterns change or when resources fluctuate.

An off-grid community can only be built with a collective effort, a focus on long-term viability, and a dedication to reliance on local resources. Fostering a resilient and harmonious living environment where individuals may thrive and positively impact each other and the natural world requires an emphasis on communication, sustainable practices, skill-sharing, collaboration, and inclusivity.

The Strength of Collaborative Survival Efforts

Collective action and mutual aid are the pillars of survival coalitions. The resilience and ability to overcome adversity of individuals or groups is considerably increased when they band together to tackle problems, share resources, and work towards a shared goal.

Successful survival coalitions draw on the complementary abilities of their members. Together, we can solve difficult issues more efficiently than any one person could do on their own. Because of the varied backgrounds and experiences represented on the team, they can approach problems from more angles and with more originality.

Together, people can respond to and coordinate during emergencies much more quickly. Communities that work together can better respond to emergencies like natural disasters, pandemics, or other threats, help those in need, and adjust to new conditions.

When members of a group work together, they develop friendships and trust in one another via their shared experiences and efforts. Because of this shared experience, people are more likely to support one another and form closer relationships with their peers.

Working together to stay alive encourages generosity and ingenuity. When resources are limited, a group can accomplish more by pooling their efforts. This benefits everyone involved.

Working together to survive has the added benefit of everyone learning from one another. Knowledge and understanding are easily shared and gained when people with varied backgrounds and expertise come together. As a result of this ongoing dialogue, the community becomes more robust and flexible, allowing its members to acquire new knowledge and adjust to shifting conditions.

Working together to survive can give you confidence and independence. Individuals' belief in their skills is bolstered, and the group's resilience is increased when members work together to find solutions to issues and provide emotional support to one another.

When people work together, they can better bear the psychological toll of surviving adversity. Meeting adversity as a community strengthens bonds, lessens the impact of individual struggles, and boosts emotional and mental health.

In addition, working together to survive isn't limited to times of crisis. Sustainable communities and practices are often the result of such efforts. Communities working together can implement long-term solutions in food security, renewable energy, and environmental stewardship.

The power of group survival strategies comes from the realization that more can be accomplished when people and groups work together. Collaborative survival efforts produce a strong and adaptable strategy for overcoming problems and thriving in a changing world through mutual support, leveraging collective knowledge and resources, and promoting a feeling of community.

Bartering and Trading in a Self-Sufficient Community

Bartering and trading become crucial economic activities in a self-sufficient community without a central bank or government to issue currency. When everyone in society grows their food and makes their products, bartering and trading become essential ways to acquire necessities that aren't produced locally.

When two people engage in a bartering transaction, they trade products and services directly instead of exchanging money. Members of society can barter their wares of surplus for necessities. Suppose one person has an overabundance of veggies from their garden, and another has an overabundance of eggs from their chickens. In that case, they can benefit from direct trade by exchanging these products instead of exchanging money.

Trading with one another encourages initiative and creativity. Cooperation and interdependence are encouraged, as is the effective use of one's abilities and those of others. By reducing the demand for expensive imported goods, bartering helps a community become more self-sufficient.

However, trading is an even more intricate system of exchanging products and services between several parties. Community currencies or tokens may be used in some trading situations but are not required. Members can bring their wares and services to regular markets or trading events hosted by the community.

When people engage in commerce, they increase their possibilities for acquiring the commodities and services they require. Allowing people to specialize in producing what they are good at and trading for what they need promotes economic diversity in the community.

Bartering and trading in a self-sufficient society also encourage the sharing of skills and the development of specialization. By knowing they can rely on their neighbors to provide their basic requirements, people can devote their time and energy to becoming experts in fields that interest them. Productivity and efficiency are both improved by the division of labor.

Bartering and trading within a self-sufficient society also foster a strong sense of community. Intimate communication and sharing between group members strengthens bonds and increases appreciation for one another's efforts.

Though essential to self-sufficient societies, bartering and trading only solve some problems. When the direct trading of particular commodities and services becomes impractical, other systems, such as community currencies and time-based trade systems, are developed.

In sum, a self-sufficient society's economic and social structure benefits greatly from bartering and trading. They encourage people to take care of their own needs and those of their neighbors without resorting to conventional currency or outside markets, and they strengthen the bonds within communities.

1. **If you haven't already done so, scan the QR code at the beginning of the book** and download THE BEST SURVIVAL DIY PROJECTS eBook + VIDEOS.

2. **Scan the QR code below and leave quick feedback on Amazon!**

SCAN ME

Conclusion

This book has covered a lot of ground, and it has covered a lot of ground well. It has shown us how to live peacefully with nature and create a thriving, self-sufficient society. In this book, we have explored the fundamental ideas and methods that enable people to live sustainably and resiliently while remaining independent of conventional utility infrastructure.

Our journey of learning to live off the grid has been one of resourcefulness and environmental responsibility, from the realm of shelter and accommodation, where we learned to build temporary and permanent structures using natural and recycled materials, to the realm of water sourcing and purification, where we learned to harness the power of rainwater and implement effective filtration techniques.

Aware of the need for ethical and responsible methods of food procurement that do not compromise wildlife or ecosystems, we investigated sustainable hunting and fishing practices. Off-grid gardening, foraging for wild delicacies, and mastering the art of food preservation allowed us to ensure a year-round sustenance supply.

When we started experimenting with making our tools and equipment, we quickly learned the importance of these improvised implements and how well they complemented our off-the-grid way of life. In the interest of health and safety, we looked into the wide world of herbal medicine and natural cures, accepting the efficacy of plants as medicine and weapons.

We learned how to start fires without matches or lighters, how to find our way about without GPS, and how to adapt our methods to city life as we figured out the intricacies of off-the-grid living for ourselves.

Throughout the trip, the power of cooperative survival efforts was on full display as people helped one another, traded goods, and built a self-sufficient society out of nothing. We were guided by the ethics of off-grid survival, which emphasized our accountability to ourselves, our community, and the natural world.

As we read on, our knowledge of how to coexist peacefully with the natural world grew, and we came to appreciate the interdependence of all species and our responsibility as stewards of the planet. Sustainable techniques, resource conservation, and encouraging a cooperative mindset were the keys that allowed us to discover the genuine core of off-grid survival.

Let us, as we reach the end of this voyage, take with us the lessons learned here and always value a healthy equilibrium between individual freedom and collective accountability. May we incorporate these teachings into not only our quest for off-the-grid existence but also our daily lives so that the good we do has an even greater impact on the world.

May we find the strength to act on these realizations and create a world where nature thrives, communities prosper, and peace between humanity and the planet lasts for future generations.

1. **If you haven't already done so, scan the QR code at the beginning of the book** and download THE BEST SURVIVAL DIY PROJECTS eBook + VIDEOS.

2. **Scan the QR code below and leave quick feedback on Amazon!**

SCAN ME

Printed in Great Britain
by Amazon

43345347R00059